Stop Freaking Out About Retirement

SECOND EDITION

ISBN 978-1-7341130-0-6

Stop Freaking Out About Retirement

SECOND EDITION

How to Reach New Goals and Enjoy
Your Life When Work Ends

by Carolina Osorio M.D.

Contents

Introduction

" *Do not let your fire go out, spark by irreplaceable spark in the hopeless swamps of the not-quite, the not-yet, and the not-at-all. Do not let the hero in your soul perish in lonely frustration for the life you deserved and have never been able to reach. The world you desire can be won. It exists. It is real. It is possible. It is yours.*"

—Ayn Rand

You and You Alone

What brings you to this book?

My best bet is that you are here because you are either considering retiring or you are into your first year of retirement and you are feeling anxious—as if you will lose your mind if you cannot control the feelings you are having about this big transitional time. It may be that your expectations about retirement have not been met. Or it may be that now, when you have the time to do everything you once thought retirement would bring you—traveling or spending time with friends and family—you find yourself wanting to do the opposite, and just be alone.

Perhaps you feel alone because other people in your circle have retired and you have never heard them talk about how difficult this has been for them. Maybe you shared these feelings with one or two of your closest friends without getting reassurance from them. You are probably feeling there must be something wrong with you. And perhaps you feel ashamed to be experiencing these thoughts and feelings.

But you are also here because you feel that time is short—I mean, time does not wait, right? You know this very well. Every hour, every day, every month is precious. They will not come back to you and you are losing some hope about how retirement can look for you. Perhaps you are missing out on grandkids, or golf tournaments or whatever you once enjoyed or were looking forward to, because you're spending too much time worrying. In spite of having a good relationship with family members and friends who have been very supportive to you, now you may be finding that you just want to be by yourself. Your life has been all about work (the average person spends 90,000 hours at work over a lifetime)—days filled with a busy schedule, time off catching up, your mind always on the "go-go-go." For some, it included raising kids, taking care of family and, for many, helping with grandkids as well. So now, having been left idle with no structure and no schedule, you may feel you are in totally new and unknown territory.

You may be thinking that you have all that it is needed in life—your basic needs are covered and a little extra is left to enjoy other things—or perhaps finances start to become a bigger concern to you. You don't quite feel right. You may find yourself unable to sleep at night (a study conducted by Dave Ramsey showed that 56 percent of Americans lose sleep thinking about retirement).[1] Sleeplessness, then, can make you feel impatient and perhaps snappy from time to time. Then you feel guilty for doing that to people who care about you. You feel guilty because your family and friends request your presence and you do not feel up to it. You are home with a lot of time left to do nothing and that can make anyone spiral down the rabbit hole. This can launch a vicious and negative cycle and as time passes it can begin to feel more intense and much more unpleasant. But again, reaching out feels impossible because someone might pass judgment, and you really think no one else has felt the same. Or you might start noticing that things which never bothered you before are now making you emotional and wanting to isolate yourself because you do not want others to see your vulnerability. There is nothing wrong with this feeling. Many people experience it. But it is actually not healthy and can lead you to remain stuck.

In the midst of anxious feelings, it is easier just to stay where we are because even though it is uncomfortable,

[1] https://www.daveramsey.com/research/stress-anxiety

it is our comfort zone. But growth does not happen here. It requires personal strength to put your wishes for change into action. The fact that you have decided to read this book and take on the work of continuing to develop yourself, however, shows enormous strength and determination, and I am very proud of you!

Let me be clear, there are many others in the same boat. I know them, I have worked with them. I have empowered them. There is no reason why you cannot do it as well. No matter how you are feeling today. You may not feel like this time in your life is "blissful," but I believe that you can get there. I 100-percent believe that you can transform a retirement that feels lonely and empty into something meaningful, enjoyable, and peaceful—into a time when you can build your resilience because, regardless of age and time, the fact that we are alive is all that is necessary to face adversity. Age may bring some more challenges, but age also gives us something precious that no other thing in life can give us, and that is wisdom. I plan to help you tap into your own wisdom, bringing it into your awareness, in order to help you create a retirement life where everything you do has a purpose and is meaningful because it aligns perfectly with your values. Each one of us is unique and wonderfully made. That is why there is not a one-size-fits-all for this process.

So many people think they have dealt with their past but later are surprised to find thoughts and emotions re-emerging and flooding them. It is very common for this to happen during the transition to retirement. Often, we don't realize the impact something has had on our lives because we are so busy, and actually many times we use that busy-ness as a coping mechanism to avoid the discomfort of experiencing the pain from prior negative experiences. Traumas from the past are not necessarily nightmarish. They can be experiences that appear small to others, or patterns of experiences that accumulate over years, but these may have a huge impact on our experience—things like strict parents, being a latch-key child, deaths of loved ones through the years, and experiences during military service are just a few. But there are two things the past is good for: to learn from and to remind you of the good times.

But You Are Not Alone

In our society, there is a general belief that once you hit retirement you are leaving your best days behind. This idea alone causes a great deal of existential anxiety as we approach retirement age. The concept that an individual's life progression culminates in a phase called "old age" is a relatively recent development that began in the second half of the 19th century, when older individuals were lumped into a single category of "the aged." Prior to this time, many different cultures viewed growing older on an individual basis that did not necessarily correlate with a set age. I believe we need to go back to that. I have seen people retire in their 50s while others do so in their 70s, and there are many different reasons why one chooses to retire sooner or later.

The belief that one's best days are over at retirement derives in part from the fact that careers give us purpose and a sense of meaning. So, retirement might mean leaving that purpose behind. Like you, I have worked hard during a meaningful career, and I understand how leaving this behind may spur an identity crisis. In my career as a psychiatrist working with older adults, I have heard the same themes expressed by many people in the early days of retirement. I've brought these themes together in this book to validate the feelings of readers going through similar things, and to suggest a way out of anxiety and into an even greater enjoyment of life.

I have had the privilege of working for the past eight years with older adults with all different kinds of problems—some with severe problems and some with problems that only required coaching for them to be free and grow. I have worked with many people who face the same or similar challenges that you are facing today as you retire. You are not alone; I can tell you this with all honesty. I've been with them; I have helped them, and I have received beautiful messages of thank you from them because I have coached them into a life of freedom.

Let me work with you on this. I have done it, and if you have an open mind and a desire to keep growing, if you can accept my help and absorb the process, just as a little child absorbs all the information that is given to him or her in order to grow, you also will grow. There is no need to waste more time. We know how precious every day is. All that we have is the present. Because the past is gone and the future we do not know. So, let's start this right now.

What Are Your Goals for These Years?

To stop freaking out about retirement, to stop spiraling in anxiety, and to break out of your self-imposed isolation, you will need to set new goals. These do not have to be grand. To help you determine your goals, the best place to start is to do an assessment of your current status, which will help you clearly set a baseline of where you are. We will spend some time in this book on exercises of self-discovery which will help you explore different areas of your life. Through this introspection, you will gain clarity that will help in guiding you toward your desired goals. I will start by talking about the importance of each area, and I will provide time for you to do a self-assessment of each of these. Once you know your baseline, you have a starting point, and it will be much easier to develop a road map into freedom and empowerment.

To give you a better idea of the journey you are about to embark on with this book, I have organized the content around the four pillars of the bio-psycho-socio-spiritual model. This model, which is how I was trained in medicine, is also called the whole-person-centered view, because it incorporates perspectives on the physical body, the mind, one's social context, and spirituality.

When we are confronted with feelings of anxiety, nervousness, feeling overwhelmed, sadness, guilt, shame, and fears, there is no magic bullet but, instead, a process that we need to go through by diving into all these areas that make a person whole. We will start with your personal assessment of where you fit in this model by doing exercises of self-discovery. Doing the lonely work to gain clarity on who you are as a human being, what your strengths are, knowing what's possible for you, and how you are defining your life's efforts, is foundational for pursuing your best during this first year of retirement.

Your dream of enjoying retirement can begin when you follow the steps in this book. A life of freedom and empowerment, equipped with better tools to overcome difficulties as they arise, will be your result.

Life does not end when you are in your 40s, 60s, or even 80s—life ends when you give up. Each decade that is granted to us is a time to pause to reflect, to reinvent, to create. There is pain at any stage, and there is enjoyment as well. Do not allow what society tells you retirement is or should be determine your own path. You and only you will walk in those shoes. You have this opportunity to transform fear into freedom. This transitioning into retirement is the perfect time to pause. Use eight weeks to recalibrate the compass that will direct you through this stage.

Through Knowledge and with a Heart of Service

I am not your age, and I have not retired, so you might be wondering how in the world I could help you with what you are facing today. You might think, how could I be equipped to give you tools and a foundation for you to start shifting into freedom and a meaningful retirement. Do I understand what you are going through? This is a perfectly appropriate question.

I would be very surprised if you did not have all of these doubts. Actually, I strongly believe that we should not believe everything at face value. We must have an inquisitive mind and understand how others can help us through very sensitive matters such as our own purpose in life, or our own health during times of transition.

So, I want you to know that I can indeed help you. I have already done this with other people in the same situation as you are in now. And I have successfully done so.

Let me start with some history. I was raised in a third-world country in South America—Colombia. Growing up there, I was very close to my grandparents. I spent many years of my childhood around them and developed a strong connection and a deep love for them. That love that I got from them triggered a series of emotions and developed a great force in me that drew me to focus my career on helping people in their later decades of life.

My father's dad died by suicide. When the tragedy took place, I was young and I loved him. The true reason for his death was hidden from me, and I understand this was to protect me as I was a child and I had a strong attachment to him. Later I came to find the truth. As I write this, I wonder if you could imagine how I felt. Maybe yes or maybe not. I was saddened, I was angry.

I knew my grandfather carried something inside him. I knew he never talked about this because he wanted to prove he was the strong man of the family. I knew also that he never talked about it out of shame, because of the stigma, that huge barrier that still today is present in almost every single cultural group in the world, but especially with males in their later decades of life. There is this culturally prescribed stoicism that gives us the message that talking about our thoughts and feelings is a sign of weakness. But this is the wrong message. I can see in retrospect that my grandfather was in the midst of a perfect storm: stoicism, fear of being seen as weak by showing feelings and emotions, being a male in his 70s. The storm hit home, and it hit with a great deal of pain.

At that time, I did not know how I was going to bring change, how I could help, I just knew that I had to do something. So, time passed, life kept going on, but I learned that the terrible experience that my family went through, the way my grandfather died, was something that could have been totally avoided. A situation like this should never have to happen. This case is a very extreme one, but it is often through intense pain that our lives are shaped and we are inspired into convictions and true callings.

As I grew, I decided to go to medical school, and another life-changing event showed me that my mission was to help others later in life. What was about to happen you may think was pure coincidence (I do not believe in coincidence, but that is not the main issue here). I was designated to work in an assisted living facility during one of my clinical rotations. At that time, I had the honor to work with a 90-year-old man for one month, a man who would instill in me a seed that would lead me to what I do today (yet another of those deep experiences). My responsibilities included meeting with him once a week and writing down his psychological development. This was part of my work in human development.

He was a retired physician. I got to know him well and to understand the challenges that he was going through. Basically, he was a widower and had no living family. He never had children, and all his family had already passed away. At the time when I was with him, he was living in a private room at the assisted living facility. He was legally blind and required assistance with some of his activities of daily living, but overall, he was pretty independent. He shared with me that all his life he had worked really hard because he knew at some point he was going to retire from medicine. He had enjoyed a great deal the service of helping others through their illnesses. Part of him wanted to retire but the other part of him was not happy about doing so. His career had become his identity. Ceasing to do what he was so devoted to doing meant losing who he was. But he also thought that retirement was going to give him the opportunity of spending time with his wife doing things they could never do before because he was working. Sadly, his wife died, he retired, and he started to isolate and got depressed. We talked about meaning, purpose, identity, faith, and all the things that make us human.

At that point I felt a great deal of frustration, and to be honest, I felt anger. Not the same anger I felt when I knew my grandfather died by suicide but nevertheless anger. You may ask why. Well, the thing is that I honor every individual who has worked hard all their lives. And seeing first-hand how someone can enter into a time of his life without the support, the guidance, and the help that was needed to overcome the difficulties to navigate such a change later in life—after all that one person had done through his life, the service and the contributions he had made—it was just too unfair, and totally wrong in my eyes. And ever since I had that interaction, I was reminded of those early feelings of a greater calling to work for those who are entering their later years, which drove me to do the work I do today.

The power of discrimination toward older adults that exists all over the world was very clear to me, and as long as I can, I will work hard, because after all those years of contribution, you deserve to enjoy and be better equipped to confront life. It is not necessary for you to suffer alone. In the worst cases, people may develop a severe mental health problem such as depression, like my grandfather, just because there is no one out there competent to help them move forward. How is it that we as a society suddenly lose any memory of or respect for the purpose that one person has in our community just because they turned a particular age?

I moved to the United States to pursue a specialization in psychiatry and then a sub-specialization in geriatric psychiatry, which encompasses the care of older adults and the prior experiences that led them to be who they are. There are specific differences when we deal with changes of life as we go through our 60th decade and ahead, from how our biology changes, to our mindset, emotions, spirituality, and social factors. I found out that there was not much support to help people entering the changes later in life.

I came to Loma Linda, California, where I continue to practice, and I developed a mental health intensive outpatient program specifically to help people overcome depression and anxiety. As the months went by, I saw a common theme for the people who were coming to the program. For some of them, transitioning into retirement was the stressor that led them to feel depressed or severely anxious. But I saw the dramatic change they went through after completing this program. Then I started questioning if there were more people struggling with the concept of retirement who were not necessarily depressed or struggling with severe anxiety. I knew deep in my heart that not everyone needed the level of care I was offering at my program. And a light bulb turned on and just with that thought I decided to write this book. I want to reach a bigger community; I want everyone to have the opportunity to be the best version of themselves and to use this powerful cathartic moment that occurs while we undergo big transitions in life.

There are three main reasons why I decided to do this work. First, because we all deserve to overcome difficulties, to have a life of peace and freedom after a long journey of hard work. I believe the later years are a time to reinvent yourself and do things that were sacrificed because you were taking care of a job, of a family, of daily life. Transitions late in life are different from those experienced when someone is in their 20s, 30s, or 40s; the challenges are not the same. Very few of us who have trained in the unique psychosocial factors of transitioning into the older years, or have been touched by interactions and relations with older adults, can truly understand the differences.

Second, because I want you to know you are not alone, that there are many others who have been in the same situation you are in now. I know this because I have worked with them, and today they are living retirement at their best. One person once wrote to me, "I thank you for helping bring my bright world after dark days had found me. You have been so kind to me and you gave me the motivation to work on my books." Another person I worked with wrote, "Thank you for giving my life back, you are wonderful, knowledgeable, caring and personable. I thank god for you and your passion for helping others." These are just two examples. It is knowing that I can help that inspires me to write this book.

Third, because you don't need to go down the rabbit hole. There is no excuse for allowing these thoughts and emotions to lead you into really bad outcomes such as developing depression, which is a terrible disease that tears apart lives and families. And I know first-hand that if we do not intercede early enough, there is a risk for this to happen.

I decided not to be a passive observer of this big elephant in the room—the discrimination against age that now has been normalized and which we call ageism. If I can help you move ahead and get unstuck and thrive in retirement, then we will build bigger communities of retirees succeeding and supporting each other when adversity knocks on the door.

My training, my clinical experience, and my own personal journey all have contributed to making my decision to write this book. You are at the center, because I believe in you and the amazing life that is ahead of you.

I am determined to be a voice, to be a link to facilitate other people, people like you, in living fully during this amazing time in life—and when I say amazing, it is because I truly and honestly believe in this statement. I made sure I trained and I practiced because I believe in outstanding work, and I believe that in order to help others one needs to be well informed, have the correct knowledge, be competent, and have the life experience that gives a deep sense of meaning to the work one does. I have gained a life's worth of experience through every interaction I had with the people I have worked with. I have learned through their stories, through their pain, and through their victories. I have been touched. My colleagues at work constantly tell me that I must stick around so that I can help them navigate their lives when retirement comes. I find that to be reassuring—that what I do indeed changes lives, and I do it with a heart of service, with knowledge and expertise.

Frame Your Work

> 66 You don't have to be a genius or a visionary or even a college graduate to be successful. You just need a framework and a dream. "
>
> —Michael Dell

You now have this book, but you will also need to get yourself a journal. There is a big selection of journals out there. You can buy just a regular notebook, or maybe something fancier with a cover you like. But when you go to get one, this is what I want you to do. Think about who you are, what you represent, get in tune with your philosophy of life, then buy that journal which will represent all of that. If a plain notebook will make it for you, go for it. This is all about you. Some people like to create their own cover. There are journals that are structured and that have different sections in which to write or draw different things. You can get one of those as well, but make sure you will have space to put down randomness, flow, creativity. One thing your journal will need to have is a space for gratitude. We will talk more about this in another chapter. If you enjoy creative writing, if you like to color or draw, or even if you have no experience at this, go get some colors, markers, whatever can give you a way to enjoy the process more, or maybe you're happy with just a pencil.

Now that you are equipped with your book and your journal, you will need to find a space with no distractions, where you can be totally comfortable and focused. Whatever that space is, reserve it for a daily meeting with yourself. This is a must. No exceptions.

It is time to start the journey into growth and optimization of who you are. This is what is going to happen. First and foremost, we will discuss the concept of awareness which then will be followed by the four pillars I mentioned earlier—the Bio, Psycho (psyche), Social, Spiritual model.

The first pillar, which we will call Bio, refers to the biology of your body. Here is where you learn how to take care of the vehicle you have been granted to navigate life. You will learn the concept of health span and the tools to increase the chance of being healthier as long as you can.

The second pillar, called Psycho, refers to your psyche, which encompasses the soul, emotions, personality, the totality of elements forming the mind. As this is hard to address since it is so broad, we will further divide it into Mindset and Emotions. We will be spending more time in this pillar. As you learn about mindset, you will find ways to break negative cycles and replace them with positive ones. We will debunk the concept of optimism. Also, you will learn about expectations and beliefs, because they are key factors that affect how we feel and our outcomes in life. Moving forward, you will learn how the brain works, how it makes you spend more time on your negative thoughts and how you will be able to change that. But that will require work for life. The fact that the brain can change its own circuits and pathways through thought and activity is one of its most important features. This is backed by rigorous research from the scientific and medical fields. Your brain will come more resourceful. You will also understand why we have knee-jerk reactions to different stimuli in the environment and how you can tune down the system in your brain that makes you react with fear and anxiety. In this step, you will be doing exercises to apply the concepts to your life. This will be followed by work on your emotions and behaviors. This next step will be bringing into your awareness past experiences that have left you with feelings that are keeping you stuck. Mainly we will focus on guilt, shame, and regret.

Now it is time to lay some ground work. The next step will help you create new SMART goals. But there is a caveat to this goal setting. You will learn to create goals that align to your personal values and your philosophy in life. If your goals do not match with these, you will not likely follow through. And this is another thing you will need to be constantly working on, it does not end when you finish reading this book. I will provide an exercise to help you start formulating those goals.

The last two pillars are interdependent. You will see how your spirituality and your social aspect have a lot to do with one another. Spirituality has to do with the meaning of your life, the meaning you bring during this time of transition into retirement. Without meaning there will be a big void. That void can lead you to negative feelings and negative behaviors that will impact your life down the road and this will impact your ability to build community. By then we will start to explore different ideas on how to create a life of purpose through the contribution to the well-being of others. If you get in touch with this, it can be a big source of passion for you. By the end of this step we will talk about gratitude and all the benefits it has when we put this into practice on a daily basis.

Once you finish the book, you must continue to work through every day. Your life can be divided into retirement before the book and after the book. Or stuck at retirement versus joy and freedom during retirement.

Let's begin!

" *New beginnings are exciting! They become exciting to us because they offer the promise of hope, the anticipation of change in our lives, and the prospect that our dreams will indeed come true!* "

—Squire Rushnell, *When God Winks on New Beginnings*

Be Aware

IN THE BEGINNING...

At the beginning of this work, we have to focus on something you may not be aware of. That is how unaware of our selves we are during most of our lives.

I can tell you first hand that one of the privileges I have in working with people that are transitioning in life is that it has helped me realize how unaware I was of so many things in my life and how much sense everything made once I became aware of them. It made perfect sense to understand why I was doing the work I was doing when I realized that early in life, I had painful situations that were related to people I loved the most, my grandparents. I now totally get it. My passion, my calling, was planted by these early life experiences and that give me even greater purpose and meaning in life rather than just doing the work because I have to work.

Being aware means being conscious of your thoughts, memories, feelings, sensations, and the environment.

We live in such a fast-paced society that we end up doing so many things automatically that our thoughts, memories, feelings, and sensations are ignored.

Then you are confronted with your first year into retirement, you are left with tons of time that is no longer filled with things that can distract your mind. And during this time these experiences start to become part of your awareness and you do not know how to deal with them, and you start freaking out.

Awareness can mean different things. The awareness I am talking about is that state of being conscious and having the ability to perceive, feel, and know how external factors may be contributing to how you feel. If at the end of this book you only developed awareness into the different steps that affect how you are living your retirement, then I can say that the job was done. But I know it will be more than that.

Part of being aware has to do with being able to sit down and reflect—to take a pause in the middle of the day and think things through. Having self-awareness means you understand your personality (including your weaknesses and strengths), your thoughts and beliefs, your emotions, and your motivations. When you have better awareness into yourself it will be easier for you to understand others and how they perceive you.

Becoming more self-aware is a step in the creation of the life that you want, and this is even more important now. As you will learn, the foundation that holds up the four pillars that you will build through this book is nothing other than self-awareness. Becoming self-aware is what will enable you to make changes in the direction for your future as a retiree.

First, we need to set a baseline. We will start with some questions that will open the door to awareness and insight.

In your journal, write down your answers to the following questions:

- *What do you love about your current life?*
- *What would you love to see more of in your life? And why?*
- *What are you good at?*
- *What would you like to see less of in your life? And why?*

· *Think of people you admire. What are the traits you most admire in them?*

Do not overthink your answers—it is best to answer with the first feeling and thought that comes to you. When you finish this book, come back to this page and read your answers out loud. Reflecting on them will help you realize the shift you have made.

Let's begin with a personal assessment.

Please take time to read the following statements and choose the best answer for how you feel this relates to your current state in life.

EMOTIONAL / CHARACTER / PERSONAL GROWTH (OPTIMISM / CONFIDENCE)

I know the values I live by.

NOT AT ALL ———————————— ABSOLUTELY
1   2   3   4   5   6   7

I know the virtues I hold.

NOT AT ALL ———————————— ABSOLUTELY
1   2   3   4   5   6   7

I feel confident about myself.

NOT AT ALL ———————————— ABSOLUTELY
1   2   3   4   5   6   7

ROMANTIC RELATIONSHIP / FAMILY

I have (know what I want for) a great love relationship.

Not at all ――――――――――――――― Absolutely
　　　1　　2　　3　　4　　5　　6　　7

SOCIAL LIFE

I am good at giving and experiencing love (from partner, friend, loved one).

Not at all ――――――――――――――― Absolutely
　　　1　　2　　3　　4　　5　　6　　7

I have high quality social relationships.

Not at all ――――――――――――――― Absolutely
　　　1　　2　　3　　4　　5　　6　　7

SPIRITUAL

I have clear spiritual beliefs and I can explain them clearly.

NOT AT ALL ———————————————— ABSOLUTELY
      1   2   3   4   5   6   7

I have a spiritual community.

NOT AT ALL ———————————————— ABSOLUTELY
      1   2   3   4   5   6   7

HEALTH AND FITNESS (SLEEP / EATING / EXERCISE)

I am satisfied with the way I look and feel when it comes to my health and fitness.

NOT AT ALL ———————————————— ABSOLUTELY
      1   2   3   4   5   6   7

I dedicate enough time to my health and fitness (exercise, meal prep, etc).

NOT AT ALL ———————————————— ABSOLUTELY
      1   2   3   4   5   6   7

FINANCES AND MONEY

I feel I have an abundant financial state.

NOT AT ALL ——————————————— ABSOLUTELY
1   2   3   4   5   6   7

I feel confident in the way I make financial decisions and planning.

NOT AT ALL ——————————————— ABSOLUTELY
1   2   3   4   5   6   7

FUN AND RECREATION (QUALITY OF LIFE)

I can enjoy hobbies and I am confident that I know what brings me joy.

NOT AT ALL ——————————————— ABSOLUTELY
1   2   3   4   5   6   7

I devote enough time to the activities that bring me joy.

NOT AT ALL ——————————————— ABSOLUTELY
1   2   3   4   5   6   7

LONGEVITY

I am working today on the above areas with the goal of making the most out of what is ahead in life.

NOT AT ALL ——————————— ABSOLUTELY
1   2   3   4   5   6   7

BONUS QUESTION:

I have a life vision.

NOT AT ALL ——————————— ABSOLUTELY
1   2   3   4   5   6   7

PILLAR 1:
Bio - Biology

Recovery Time Tools

> " The body needs its rest, and sleep is extremely important in any health regimen. There should be three main things: eating, exercise, and sleep. All three together in the right balance make for a truly healthy lifestyle."

—Rohit Shetty

What is your first thought when you hear "It is recovery time"? For me, the first image that comes to my mind is of someone who had an intense training or intense working hours and now has to rest. You might be wondering why it is important to talk about recovery when you are dealing with this life transition.

The idea behind this is nothing less than learning the importance of lifestyle for optimization of who you want to become. There are a lot of people talking about this, and a lot of information out there, but it just seems to be way too much and too generalized.

To live an outstanding life full of joy and to pursue your best version yet, you *do* need to be alive. Here is where paying attention to your health is so important. This is why recovery time is crucial. Not only this, the quality of your life, how much energy you have, your vitality, are all deeply dependent on your health. Eating, exercise, sleep, and rest are big components to focus on to make the most of your health. In this area also lies the very important concept of recovery. This is key to exponential growth, just as it is the key for athletes to maintain high-level performance. For the rest of us non-athletes, it is the time to rest, meditate, process, sleep, and reset our bodies.

We are living longer than ever. Life span has increased significantly, and currently in the US, life expectancy is 78.6 years. People are living longer for many different reasons—vaccinations and improvements in medical care among others. But in my experience, even though we want to extend our years, most important is the quality of those years. We want to live those years free of chronic illness. You may be taking multiple medications in your 60s for a variety of medical problems, going in and out of doctors' offices throughout the year. Or you may be in your 80s going out with your friends on bike rides, completely healthy, going to your doctor just for preventive care. And that is what we call your health span. But while people are taking more interest in aging and life span, very little is being said about health span. Health span is defined as the period of one's life that is free from serious disease. Serious diseases are those that lead to death or significant loss of independence. Some of these are cancer, heart disease, Alzheimer's disease and other dementias, long-term uncontrolled diabetes and high blood pressure.

And this is really my message here, because I want you to live this new chapter in your life in the best way possible. And we cannot do that if we do not take care of our bodies, this vehicle that has been given to us to navigate life. You cannot go on the freeways at 65 miles per hour for days and days with a broken car. I bet you take really good care of your car. The same thing is going to happen with your body, so we better start getting serious about this. It is never too late. Because all we have is this day, this present moment, to start implementing small changes.

Most of us will get sick at any given time in our lives. They are certain conditions that really can be prevented, while others cannot. But we have the power to implement action to decrease the risk of getting chronically sick. There is a lot of information about lifestyle changes that could delay most of the serious diseases. Diabetes type 2 is a great example. About 75 percent of diabetes type 2 can be prevented and improved just by lifestyle interventions. You can have a lot of power over the biology of your body by applying the concepts that lifestyle medicine teaches us. So, we will go into detail about what the interventions are that can promote a longer health span during your retirement years.

TOOL #1: MOVEMENT

There is no question that physical activity as well as food are totally misused in our society. We spend hours and hours sitting. Even though technology is imperative for our society to progress it can also hinder us. So, in the case of physical activity, technology has had in part a negative effect. Nowadays everything can happen just by using our fingertips. I remember back in the day when we did not have TV remote control, we had to stand up, walk toward the TV, and change the channel, and then go back to the chair. Just an example. So, these little things add up to the point where we really are not moving much. At the same time, we benefit from things like activity trackers which help us count our steps. It is within constant movement where health lies at the most basic. To help you better understand this concept, let me give you some clear definitions.

Physical activity is defined as any bodily movement produced by skeletal muscles that results in energy expenditure. Physical activity in daily life can be categorized into occupational, sports, conditioning, household, or other activities. Exercise is a subset of physical activity that is planned, structured, and repetitive and has as a final or an intermediate objective the improvement or maintenance of physical fitness.

Physical fitness is a set of attributes that are either health- or skill-related. Everyone performs physical activity in order to sustain life; however, the amount is largely subject to personal choice and may vary considerably from person to person as well as for a given person over time. So, if you do not have a structured time for exercise, this is a place where you can start to increase your physical activities. Maybe take the stairs more often. Or park your car a little farther away each time when you go places. Maybe take laps inside your house.

In contrast with physical activity, which is related to the movements that people perform, physical fitness is a set of attributes that people have or achieve. Being physically fit has been defined as "the ability to carry out daily tasks with vigor and alertness, without undue fatigue and with ample energy to enjoy leisure-time pursuits and to meet unforeseen emergencies."[2] See

[2] Public Health Rep. 1985 Mar-Apr; 100(2): 126–131. Physical activity, exercise, and physical fitness: definitions and distinctions for health-related research. C J Caspersen, K E Powell, and G M Christenson. Available at: https://www.ncbi.nlm.nih.gov/pmc/articles/PMC1424733/

how this is super important now that you are retired? Our goal is that, upon finishing this chapter, you bring into your awareness the basic understanding of physical fitness and perhaps start to build a habit to help you move your fitness higher than where you are. Exercise has so many benefits. The way you move, the way you train—or don't—can have a great impact in your life and daily activities. Sedentary older adults definitely have a higher risk of developing chronic serious medical problems. The reserve that the body has to recover from anything, from a flu to a broken bone, is less than during their teens or 20s. Something that may happen to someone who is active may be overcome, but for someone who is sedentary, it may lead to total disability or death.

Physical activity can help improve health, reduce stress, improve pain, improve posture, increase energy, improve quality of sleep, even oxygenate the brain better, leading to better cognitive functions, better memory and the ability to do tasks.

Let's take a look at the example of chronic sitters. I've heard it said that sitting is the new smoking—in that previous generations didn't know smoking was bad, and seemingly everyone was doing it. It feels good, it's relaxing, but the truth is that if you are sitting most of your day and not really moving much, your hips get tight, and this leads to bad back posture and bad ways of moving, potentially back pain and all kinds of other small (or big) symptoms that are really a distraction from what you are trying to focus on and do—in this case enjoy your retirement. You can begin to reverse this trend by getting at least 2.5 hours of moderate movement a week.

Wherever you are in your fitness, let's start creating change right now. Begin by envisioning the outcome you want to have in this area, keeping it realistic, of course. Then, let's start bringing that vision into action. In order to do this, you will want to break it into concrete baby steps. Don't try to change everything at once. So, for example, if you literally sit all day and you do not have any dedicated time for fitness training, you may be thinking "I just have to start going to the gym." That is not specific and is very general and will therefore be harder to accomplish. Instead, you might say, "I am going to do 15 push-ups 5 days a week as soon as I wake up." We want things that are specific, matched with a timeline.

So, let's start with a very simple exercise.

- *The biggest outcome for my health and fitness is:*
- *The next baby step is:*
- *I will take this step by:*

These baby steps should feel manageable and a little scary—and you might even feel "frexcited." I love this word: a little freaking out, but mostly excited!

Once you have accomplished this one baby step then you will go on to add the second and so forth. If you commit to one baby step per week, you will have accomplished four of those by the next month.

Okay, now, because food and physical activity are interdependent and each accomplishes different things while complementing each other in sustaining your fitness and health, I will now discuss eating habits. And at the end, we will see how these two topics sync together as you pursue a more active and healthy life.

TOOL #2: FOOD

Most of us eat what is known as the SAD—Standard American Diet—which is characterized by higher quantities of processed and animal-based than plant-based foods and fats; high sugar consumption is another part of the SAD. This diet is associated with a spate of chronic diseases, as I will go into in more detail below.

There are many books and schools of thoughts about what foods to consume and what is the best diet or the best eating habits. But the reality is that if you cannot sustain those eating habits, then it is not going to work. The most important thing about changing your diet is that whatever you choose should be sustainable for you. After years of learning all about food and its connections to our brain and body, I know that the diet that yields the best benefits is plant based. However, many people find it very difficult to sustain a plant-based diet if they have not been raised this way. This has been my own experience, in any case. I have tried many different ways of being healthy, including an all plant-based diet, and it did not last very long. But this diet really has the best evidence when it comes to health benefits. So, if your diet is already plant based—terrific!!

The next set of eating habits I am going to talk about is what is called the Mediterranean diet, which has been studied widely and has a great deal of evidence of health benefits. And what also makes it appealing is that it is probably easier to follow than a strictly plant-based diet. The Mediterranean diet is largely plant based, but also includes meat, fish, and some dairy foods. Research has shown that the traditional Mediterranean diet reduces the risk of heart disease. In fact, a meta-analysis of more than 1.5 million healthy adults demonstrated that following a Mediterranean diet was associated with a reduced risk of cardiovascular mortality as well as overall mortality. The Mediterranean diet is also associated with a reduced incidence of cancer, and Parkinson's and Alzheimer's diseases. Women who eat a Mediterranean diet that includes extra-virgin olive oil and mixed nuts may have a reduced risk of breast cancer. For these reasons, most if not all major scientific organizations encourage healthy adults to adopt a style of eating like that of the Mediterranean diet for prevention of major chronic diseases.

This diet emphasizes:

- Eating primarily plant-based foods, such as fruits and vegetables, whole grains, legumes, and nuts
- Replacing butter with healthy fats such as olive oil and avocado oil
- Using herbs and spices instead of salt to flavor foods
- Limiting red meat consumption to no more than a few times per month
- Eating fish and poultry at least twice a week
- Enjoying meals with family and friends
- Drinking red wine in moderation (optional). This means no more than 5 ounces (148 milliliters) of wine daily for women (or men over age 65), and no more than 10 ounces (296 milliliters) of wine daily for men under age 65. If you're unable to limit your alcohol intake to the amounts defined above, if you have a personal or family history of alcohol abuse, or if you have heart or liver disease, refrain from drinking wine or any other alcohol.

Besides the benefits of good nutrition, the other really important side of the coin is what to avoid at all cost. So, in general, anything that is highly processed is really bad for your brain and your body, especially anything that contains added refined sugar. Unfortunately, almost everything that is packaged contains added sugar (and usually salt and unhealthy fats). I learned this a while ago because when I started to look at the ingredients of everything I was buying, to my surprise, I realized that almost anything in a package had sugar. I went to buy turkey breast and guess what? In the ingredients it said sugar! Sugar consumption has been linked to an array of diseases from cancer to cardiovascular illness to diabetes and obesity, all of which increase the likelihood of early mortality.

Don't get me wrong. Many healthful foods such as vegetables and fruits contain naturally occurring sugar. It is important to include them on your diet because they also have other nutrients needed for our health, such as fiber, vitamins, and minerals. However, processed foods usually have added refined sugar. It is these added sugars that cause health problems because they do not provide any nutritional value. This is what is called empty calories. These sugars also add an incredible amount of calories, and since refined sugars are easily digested, these foods do not keep us full for long and make us hungry more frequently. This eventually will lead to weight gain and obesity. Even if you are exercising, if you do not take away these refined sugars, you will not lose the weight. But you should also beware of items that say they have zero calories; sugar substitutes are often just as bad for our bodies. Bottom line: eat nothing processed, nothing outside of the whole food aisles.

TOOL #3: SLEEP

❝Sleep is that golden chain that ties health and our bodies together."

—Thomas Dekker

Our sleep is so neglected. We put such little emphasis on sleep as an aspect of health. And yet there is a big silent epidemic of sleepless nights. When we talk about sleep, what I mean is a restful time when you are accomplishing a lot without knowing it. It is during sleep that our brains clean the debris of the day, including waste proteins that are toxic to brain cells and that with time get stored and can produce diseases, including Alzheimer's disease. Have you heard that people with chronic insomnia are at higher risk for this disease? Well, it is true. People with insomnia also have higher risk for cardiovascular diseases. So insomnia should not be taken lightly.

While we are sleeping, a lot is going on in our bodies as well as in the brain. Sleep reduces the body's amount of stress hormones, adjusts the hormones that control appetite, and boosts the immune system.

When you are not sleeping enough, you'll probably have trouble holding onto and recalling details. That is in part because sleep plays a big role in both learning and memory. It is hard to focus when we are sleep deprived. Also, with lack of sleep people tend to have more negative emotional reactions and fewer positive ones.

There are different sources of information about how many hours a person needs for sleep. But at a minimum, humans require five and a half hours of sleep. That is what in medicine is called core sleep. A sleep cycle lasts 90 minutes. A normal night's sleep involves four of these 90-minute cycles. However, per guidelines set by the Centers for Disease Control and Prevention (CDC), as well as the National Institute of Health (NIH), the recommended daily amount of sleep for adults is a minimum of seven hours. But everyone is different. The best range is from six to eight hours of sleep.

On the other side of the coin, too much sleep also is not healthy. A study published in the European Heart Journal found that people who slept more than the recommended six to eight hours per day—including daytime naps—had an increased risk of dying and developing cardiovascular disease. Researchers found that people who slept for eight to nine hours per day had a 5 percent increased risk of developing harmful health conditions compared to people who slept for the recommended six to eight hours. The more a person slept, the more risk they had. For those who slept between 9 and 10 hours, their increased risk was 17 percent. Adults who slept more than 10 hours per day, including naps, had a 41 percent increased risk of dying or developing harmful health conditions. Additionally, researchers discovered that napping during the day was associated with an increased risk of health issues among people who slept more than six hours per night but not in people who slept fewer than six hours per night.

It all comes down to your core sleep. If you sleep five and a half hours at night, you can nap during the day. But if your core sleep is six hours or more, then I am sorry to let you know, but it would not be healthy for you to nap during the day.

It is an act of balance. So, if you need to improve your sleep time, this is the work you can start doing.

In order to develop a good sleep habit, the most important thing you need to do is to decrease the time you spend in bed until you actually fall asleep. This is called sleep latency. So, for example, if you are in bed by 8:00 at night and you have not fallen asleep by 8:30, you need to get out of bed. This is where the key to success is. Spending more time in bed makes it harder to sleep. The worst thing you can do is to go to bed early, get out of bed late, and nap during the day. My suggestion to you is to elect to stay awake rather than fighting to get back to sleep. If you wake up in the middle of the night and you cannot fall asleep within 20–30 minutes of waking up, get out of bed and do something else. Ideally, you will go to a different room and, with dim lights, try to read a book, and maybe have a cup of something warm to drink (tea for example). Also, always go to sleep and wake up at the same time. Consistency will pay off. Do not snooze the alarm button. As soon as it goes off, jump out of bed. Lastly, develop a pre-sleep routine. No computer, tablet, or cell phone two hours before bed. The blue light of these electronics activates your brain and will make it even harder for you to fall asleep.

PILLAR 2:
Psycho(e)

" For twenty years, my research has shown that the view you adopt of yourself profoundly affects the way you lead your life."

—Carol Dweck, *Mindset*

Mind Over Matter

To help you navigate this chapter, I am going to start by familiarizing you with the concept of mindset. You may have heard this term, or you may not have. Mindset is the set of attitudes that shapes the way you think of yourself—for example, how you perceive your intelligence, talents, and possibilities. Mindset is the filter you have on reality. You see how this plays a critical role in how you are feeling and behaving right now at this time in your retirement?

The way you perceive yourself through your mindset can determine whether you become the person you want to be and whether you live according to your values. This is where most training happens in the self-development world. And although mindset is a very important concept, it is only a small fraction of the whole picture. If you are only focusing on mindset, you are missing close to 80 percent of the areas that are key to a thriving life. And that is why when you have finished this book, you will not only have worked on mindset but also on every single other area that will be pivotal in your journey with me.

Dr. Carol Dweck, a Stanford University psychologist, has done a lot of research on the concept of mindset. Her research shows that there are mainly two types of mindsets: fixed and growth. A fixed mindset is one in which we believe that our talents and intelligence are fixed at birth. A typical example of someone with a fixed mindset would be someone who believed they couldn't learn a new skill at the end of their career, because they didn't see that skill as part of their type of intelligence. In this scenario, one might say, "retirement means the end of work; I will not be able to do anything anymore." A big one for me was "I can never be fit." A couple of years ago I suffered from burnout and had gained a whole bunch of weight to the point where I almost developed diabetes. My physician showed concern and was very emphatic that if I did not start working out and changing my eating habits, I would become diabetic. But I had such a fixed mindset about my ability to be fit that I felt paralyzed and stuck.

A belief that one is limited in a certain area is what defines the fixed mindset. This happens when people begin to hold false beliefs about themselves. Constructing a reality around this belief leads them to shy away from things or situations that would be challenging and could "prove" to them that they "don't have it" anymore or that "retirement is a time of decline because we are too old to start something new." It's a mindset that limits people. The fixed mindset sees small failures as proof that "I'm not smart" or "I'm not good at that." This is a limiting way of looking at challenges and failures, because instead of giving up, one could instead try to tackle the challenge again, try to learn more first, or try harder. The fixed mindset is made up of experiences and beliefs that are picked up along the way in life, and it is affected by cultural conditioning. So just think about all the messages we get in our society about retirement—maybe they are good, and that is where you feel disconnected, or maybe they imagine retirement as a time when people give up, because retirement means the end of work. This is a fixed mindset.

I am going to introduce a new term to you, which is the *psychological immune system*.[3] The immune system protects us from all kind of infections, helping our bodies not to get sick. The psychological immune system kicks in when we experience events that send

[3] This concept was developed by Harvard University social psychologist Daniel Gilbert, PhD and social psychologist Timothy Wilson, PhD, of the University of Virginia.

us into an emotional tailspin and tries to protect us from negative emotions. Putting it more simply, it is that part of your mind that keeps you safe and feeling good. For those who have a fixed mindset, the psychological immune system and experiences that support their own negative beliefs will work to keep them "safe" by retreating from new challenges. In effect, it is as if they do not believe in growth. They will put themselves in a position where they can prove that they are smart or right.

When kids with a fixed mindset had the opportunity to take a test that was challenging versus a test that was easy, they chose the easy test. Kids with a growth mindset preferred the challenging test. Some people believe you can grow your intelligence through effort. This is called a growth mindset. A person with a growth mindset believes that intelligence and talents are not fixed but are completely malleable.

Why is mindset important to you, at this point in your life?

The type of mindset a person holds has huge implications when it comes to motivation. Someone with a fixed mindset who is convinced that intelligence or talents are limited to what they got in their genes is likely to believe that success has a lot to do with talent and that some people are born to succeed and others just aren't. When it comes to deciding what to do in the face of a challenge, they will likely opt for the safest route and not face any difficulties because "they don't have what it takes," they "were not born for it." The belief that intelligence is malleable and can be increased can better equip any person for challenging tasks and matters. Knowing that effort and perseverance can make a difference is the success formula. A growth mindset creates a love for learning, for the process, that is essential in achieving goals.

I will return for a moment to my own experience of adjusting my mindset. I was so concerned with going down even more on my health. Becoming diabetic in my mind was something I was going to fight. I hired a personal trainer and little by little I started to change my eating habits and level of physical activity. It was incredibly difficult. Today when I look back I am just perplexed at where I am today and how far I came. My blood sugar levels are perfect. I have run multiple half marathons. Hello! Yes, I am still perplexed. But everything really clicked when I pushed myself to my limit and joined a team of awesome people and we ran a 200-mile relay race. That medal is placed in the middle of my office. I look at it to remind myself how much we can accomplish by changing our mindsets and overcoming negative self-beliefs. I believe in this because I am a living testimony of it.

The type of mindset a person has will set the stage for either "performance goals" or for "learning goals"—which emphasize either outcomes or process. Let's look at students, for example. A student with a performance goal will be more focused on the fear of not looking dumb, wanting to prove that they are smart, and in doing so try to avoid more challenging tasks. A student with a learning goal will be eager to take on more challenging tasks as there is more learning to do. Retirement gives you an amazing opportunity to learn and take on challenges that will make you grow and make you grittier.

People's ideas and beliefs about their own intelligence or abilities have profound effects on their motivation, effort, and the way they approach a challenge. What stands between you and the goals you want to achieve is a set of skills. People with fixed mindsets shy away from the challenge of learning and acquiring these skills because they believe that there is a ceiling in what they can learn and do. Growth mindset pushes people to challenge themselves, train themselves, and persevere to obtain the skill sets they need to reach their goals. You will have the time needed to train and to push yourself.

Science backs this up with the amazing concept of neuroplasticity that shows us how neurons (which are your brain cells), neuronal connections, and pathways all grow and develop as you learn something new, as you acquire a new skill, and as you practice a new task *throughout life*. The brain will rewire itself, and brain development does not stop when our bodies stop growing. Learning a completely new skill, something you have never done before, puts your brain to work and is known to be a protective factor against developing Alzheimer's disease dementia.

People with a fixed mindset think they can't. And they can't! People with a growth mindset will seek opportunities for growth, for learning, for new challenges. People with a growth mindset do not take a bad outcome as a failure but instead as a learning point. The point is to learn and grow, the process is what matters. For a fixed mindset what matters most is the outcome, and if the outcome was not what they expected, it is seen as failure.

WHAT DO YOU BELIEVE ABOUT YOURSELF?

You can see how your mindset can determine your expectations, right? But what is an expectation? Is it a strong belief that something will happen or be the case in the future? A belief that someone will or should achieve something? Expectations are beliefs about what needs to happen. An expectation projects you into the ideal image of yourself in the future, but since you are not there yet, you may get easily frustrated. The expectation is created by the non-acceptance of the now. You would rather be in the future than in the now. Expectations are the silent killer of your happiness. Most of us are not aware of our own expectations. They have become integrated into our belief system and we see them as the norm. Not meeting your expectations can lead to anxiety, disappointment, frustration, and low self-esteem and can even go on to destroy your passion.

So, take a few moments to reflect on what your expectations have been about this first year in retirement. Write it down so it materializes.

So, if expectations are beliefs, what are beliefs?

From the scientific perspective, there is a neuro-biological definition of belief: "Belief is a group of cells that have been connected and reinforced." When a neuronal pathway is frequently reinforced, it grows and gets stronger. For example, when you go to your favorite store from home you usually take the same road, the way you get to the store is a neuronal pathway in your brain, and with time it gets to be automatic. You put little effort into driving down the road because it is almost an automatic thing. Let's say one day the road is blocked due to road construction and you have to take a different route. This is the equivalent of building a new neuronal pathway in your brain. It takes active effort as it is a new experience, a new way of doing something. You will have to think the way through, assess for the fastest detour, etc. If you start taking that second route every day, with time that road map in your brain will become automatic—as that neuronal pathway is getting stronger.

We create pathways every time we experience something new or different. This is neuroplasticity in action. Now, I want to do an exercise with you. Think about yourself as we go through this.

WHAT ARE THE STORIES YOU TELL YOURSELF?

Let's explore the beliefs about yourself that you have been strengthening. Why? Because when we want to change, more frequently than not, we end up battling ourselves to change. We are our own biggest enemies. This is not to blame you, but rather to prepare you. You may have heard of limiting beliefs; these are the lies that you believe about yourself that keep you stuck. These are the stories we want to uncover so that we can start tackling them. These are the behaviors you desperately want to understand and change, like procrastination or self-sabotage. Examples may be binge eating to cope, relapsing on substance abuse, or pushing away people that we actually care for. We all do things like this, and you likely can name at least five of them. In your journal, write down at least five behaviors and associated beliefs about yourself that have been holding you back this past year.

Writing this down might feel uncomfortable, and that is okay, it is expected. But this exercise is about awareness and self-discovery. Before we can actually do something, we need to start by *identifying where to start. All your behavior is driven by a story you tell yourself. Behavior is created by thoughts. So, if you change the thoughts or stories you repeat about yourself, this can lead to changes in behavior. Some common stories that can hold you back may sound like this:*

- *"I'm too old."*
- *"It is too late."*
- *"I don't have what it takes."*
- *"I don't have time."*
- *"I don't have enough money."*
- *"Other people always come first."*
- *"They will not approve of who I truly am."*
- *"I'm this way and I can't change."*
- *"I am not worth it."*

Some of this may resonate with you, or you may have a different one you tell yourself. Let's try to identify the top three stories you tell yourself.

Next, let us try to identify where each of these stories comes from. For each one of the stories you wrote above, ask yourself: "When was the first time I remember hearing this?" Ask this question aloud and write down whatever answer comes to mind without judgment.

Common examples of where the stories could have come from:

- Parents
- Partners
- Friends
- Neighbors
- Family
- Role models
- Former work peers
- Religion
- Social media
- One's negative views of oneself

Now for your turn: for each of the stories, identify the top five sources of the stories you tell yourself and list them in your journal. Next, try to answer as completely as you can the following questions about the stories you tell yourself:

- Which of these messages continue to dominate your thoughts today?

- *What is the belief you wish to work on?*
- *Is it true? Is it really true? Would friends or family say it was true about you? Can you absolutely know for sure it is true, or do you just believe it to be true based on past experiences?*
- *What is the payoff? What are the benefits of you holding on to this belief? How does it serve you?*
- *What is the cost? How does it alter who you are? How does it affect your behaviors? How does it impact your attitudes?*

Now turn the belief around, in terms of a positive message. If your belief was: "I will not be able to enjoy my retirement," then the new thought becomes: "I will enjoy my retirement."

Is it possible to hold your new thought as being true, or truer than the original belief? If you lived this new thought, what would you do differently? Write down in one sentence your new belief and write a short paragraph on how you would visualize your new life holding to that belief.

HOW DO YOU FEEL ABOUT YOURSELF?

To be able to heal, one must allow oneself to feel. The next step is to identify the feeling that is linked to each of the stories you have been telling yourself for so long. Let me tell you that most people try to avoid doing this at any point. It is very uncomfortable, but also such a huge step towards healing and becoming a better version of yourself. This is hard, and you might find yourself wanting to give up and close the book. Because it is all about the discomfort and that psychological immune system getting activated, protecting you from discomfort and preferring to keep you in a safe zone. But you are here because that is not working for you. Keep going on—don't give up.

Go back to the list you wrote above and, as you re-read it, pay attention to your body. What are the feelings that are coming up? Where do you feel them?

As the hard worker you have been, you may be very used to numbing these emotions and dealing with high-stakes/high-stress environment without flinching. If this is the case for you, this exercise might be difficult, or you may think it brings no feelings for you.

I'll encourage you to keep trying. Ask yourself aloud, "How does xyz story make me feel?" And then notice your body's response.

For some, feelings may come as a desire to drink and numb the uncomfortableness. Maybe you'll feel heaviness in your limbs. Maybe it feels like loneliness in your heart or an empty hole. Maybe anger, sadness or fear. It could also feel like a headache, upset stomach, muscle tightness, chest pressure, tingling sensations. It can even contribute to chronic pain.

This may make you feel raw, and this is okay ... we won't stay here for long ... just enough to bring awareness and be able to name each emotion.

In your journal, list at least five emotions that you feel as a result of thinking of these limiting behaviors and stories, and the areas in your body where you feel them:

I feel _____

in my _____.

THE POWER OF BELIEFS

" *Beliefs have the power to create and the power to destroy. Human beings have the awesome ability to take any experience of their lives and create a meaning that disempowers them or one that can literally save their lives.*"

—Tony Robbins

We have already defined beliefs as the neuronal pathway that is reinforced; basically, the thought we chose to believe and repeat will grow to be what we hold as a fact. A belief produces an emotion—which in turn is felt in our body. And emotion produces a story or thought—how you describe your circumstances or explain what happened. A story produces a behavior—this is the pattern of behaviors you have, how you respond to your circumstances.

But what is the source of all this? It originates with trauma. Trauma tends to be easily disregarded, especially by high achievers, hard-working individuals who have been through so much and conquered so much. But truth be told, everyone experiences trauma in their life. Traumas are experiences that mark our lives. They can be small or big. They differ from one person to the next. It might have been the experience you had while serving, and that you have successfully buried all these years of your life by working hard. But we all experience trauma in our life, which leads to forming our perception of the world, those around us, and life in general. It guides the formation of our thoughts, which is how beliefs are formed.

Tony Robbins also said that beliefs are "a feeling of absolute certainty about what something means." But "what something means" differs from person to person, and is not a universal fact, though it may feel that way to the person holding that belief.

So, how did you get here? You have to uncover what is keeping you stuck, so you can heal it, re-create the meaning it has in your life, and start living the life you want.

Let me be straightforward with you. Whatever happened to you, whatever the source is of your limiting beliefs, it was not your fault. But it is your responsibility to decide if you will stay there or not. The ball is in your court. If you are working through this book, it is because something in you resonated with the idea of taking the wheel of your life and regaining control. So, I want to empower you and encourage you to keep going.

Let us pause here to talk about a topic that will be an amazing coping skill. That is optimism.

But what is optimism? Optimism is the belief that something good is about to happen. Many times, it is associated with being soft, or being a dreamer. But optimism is actually a very important skill for successful people. Let's dive into this. There is optimism, and there is naive optimism, which some call blind optimism. Naive or blind optimism is actually a dangerous place to be—this is the person that thinks the future will turn bright soon, but who has not put any effort or work towards making it happen. This is what keeps people in bad relationships, but not doing anything about it. On the other side there is pessimism, which is the fundamental belief that something bad is about to happen. And excessive pessimism is a pattern of believing that the future will not work out. I hear this very commonly in people who are in their first year of retirement.

> ❝A pessimist sees the difficulty in every opportunity; an optimist sees the opportunity in every difficulty."
>
> —Winston Churchill

Why is optimism so important, and what does it have to do with mindset? Research shows that optimism can reduce stress levels. Optimistic people have significantly healthier lives than pessimists. Optimistic teams create more positive synergy and perform better than pessimistic ones. Optimism is at the center of mental toughness. When you are set to work on a goal, there will be hard times coming ahead. Challenges. The way you tackle them will make a difference. Here is where optimism comes into play.

Optimism goes hand in hand with awareness and is part of your mindset, because when you start to become aware of your thoughts, emotions, and sensations, things start to make more sense and then you can strengthen your optimism and you are building a more resilient mindset. And there are many things you will be doing to increase self-awareness and—guess what?—also train your optimism!

How do you train optimism? By journaling. When you start logging your awesome events, it is not about just checking a box, it is about the experience of reflecting back on them. By searching for the good in life, you become more optimistic.

So, let's dive into an exercise, and I want you to do this exercise at least daily while you finish this book. Challenge yourself to start writing down every night two awesome events that occurred that particular day. For example: It was Sunday. It had rained all week where I live. And that Sunday the sun was out and shining. I had to work that weekend. I was not thrilled about that. Anyways, when the day ended, I sat down to do some journaling. I reminded myself of the sunny and warm day we had had after a long week of rain and cold weather. It felt pretty awesome!

Peace Be with You

Right before I introduced the concept of optimism, I briefly mentioned a known factor that keeps everyone stuck, which is past traumatic experience. Let me clarify something about this term. We hear the word trauma concerning events such as shootings that have increased in our country, and it is also used to explain events that are "simpler" like an argument with your partner. So, what does trauma really mean? Are we minimizing it or blowing it up?

In truth, defining the word trauma is very challenging. Peter Levine, a leading trauma expert and the author of the best-selling book, Waking the Tiger: Healing Trauma, says, "Trauma is the most avoided, ignored, denied, misunderstood, and untreated cause of human suffering. When I use the word trauma, I am talking here about the often debilitating symptoms that many people suffer from in the aftermath of perceived life-threatening or overwhelming experiences." Trauma is personal. An event might be traumatic for one person and not necessarily for another. The response to a threat is influenced by many factors, and the two most important ones are what we call nature versus nurture. Nature would be your own set of genes and nurture the way you have been raised.

Trauma can arise from a car accident, loss of a loved one, a long and difficult divorce, and natural disasters, among others, or from repeated small abuses like critical comments from a partner. Trauma can impact us for years and we can adapt or cope with it, though not always with the most healthy skills. A commonly used coping skill is work. Yes, work as a way of coping with feelings left inside after something traumatic has happened. And then when you are confronted with retirement and losing that coping mechanism, then all those emotions start to surface.

I will quote Dr. Levine again, here. He says:

> In short, trauma is about loss of connection— to ourselves, to our bodies, to our families, to others, and to the world around us. This loss of connection is often hard to recognize, because it doesn't happen all at once. It can happen slowly, over time, and we adapt to these subtle changes sometimes without even noticing them.

These are the hidden effects of trauma, the ones most of us keep to ourselves. We may simply sense that we do not feel quite right, without ever becoming fully aware of what is taking place; that is, the gradual undermining of our self-esteem, self-confidence, feelings of well-being, and connection to life.

Our choices become limited as we avoid certain feelings, people, situations, and places. The result of this gradual constriction of freedom is the loss of vitality and potential for the fulfillment of our dreams.[4]

So, now let's dive in more on this barrier and how we can work through it, because it is necessary to make peace with your past. Why are we focusing on the past? Because it can become a huge problem, and it often does. The past can hold us back if we haven't properly healed from it. It puts a brake on our growth and advancement. It is like an anchor. To be able to move forward, one has to make peace with the past. And how do you do this, you may ask? You have to feel it in order to deal with it and heal it.

[4] https://www.dailyom.com/cgi-bin/display/librarydisplay.cgi?lid=2018

Working with people during their first year of retirement, I get to discover with them past traumas that keep them a prisoner of fear and worrying minds. Worrying minds that make them exhausted. Just to give you some examples... I was working with a person who had been in Vietnam and had experienced combat. When I started working with him, he mentioned this experience but he said that it was all in the past and had not affected him in any way in the past 40 years of his life. He then described how when he returned to civilian life, he did struggle with alcoholism but again he went back to say that he had been sober for 40 years and that was part of the past. We continued to do work, but he was not really moving forward. He was in his ninth month post-retirement and he was feeling very anxious. He loved to travel with his family in his RV, but now he was afraid of driving it. I had not given much attention to the part of his story about Vietnam until later when I was re-evaluating his improvement—better said, his very little improvement. And then it just came to me as an epiphany! I had dropped the ball on something incredibly important. I was having a session with him and all he could talk about was the pain in his back that started early in his retirement year (he already had an extensive workup for that and everything was normal). By then he already knew that his back pain was nothing more than "anxiety." So as we were talking I told him that I needed for him to describe in full detail what had happened during his time in Vietnam.

He was resistant to do it. Remember? When we feel psychological discomfort, we have the inclination to run away from it, because we are wired to do that. He did not know why I wanted to go there if we had already talked about it and he felt that was part of the past. However, he trusted in me and he knew that whatever I was doing there was a reason behind it. So, he started to describe one thing at a time. He then paused for a minute and said, "I am getting emotional here," and then he completely changed the topic, asking me a question that had nothing to do with the processing that was going on. So, I redirected him and he said: "I came down the mountain and that is when my two buddies were killed." Silence came down in the room, I could feel his discomfort. But he was not alone. I was there with him and for him. And then I said, "You have not grieved for your friends...." He had buried this huge pain deep down where he could not have access to it. His coping skill was his work.

Work so hard that there was no time for emotions. And actually, that is a message that people who live lives in survival mode have deeply ingrained—"there is no time for emotion; that is a luxury." But now, he had all the time that he never had before, and those strong emotions that he had been carrying all along were coming out.

He looked at me and said "I do not know how to grieve." He then immediately stood up and said, "My back pain is getting worse," as he bent down in an attempt to stretch his lower back. At which time I pointed out to him that as soon as he talked about this big loss and his feelings of guilt for surviving, his back pain intensified. I was able to make him aware that this emotional pain was coming out in the form of back pain. He totally agreed with that. For most people, physical pain is much more acceptable than emotional pain.

So many of us are afraid of feeling emotional pain to the point that we stuff it down, or numb it out... something I commonly see—people numbing emotions with alcohol, drugs, or work. But the reality is that the past is still there. We often think of the past even when we don't realize we do. You may be triggered to remember it by people you see, places you visit, songs, and even smells. So many things can trigger you, and that is because we have a part of our brain called the amygdala that is in charge of assigning meaning—which is emotional—to everything that happens in our life. By the time we get to adulthood, most everything around us has had some type of meaning in our lives and will trigger memories in our brain.

I have always been fascinated by the brain. Once you have a better understanding of the implications of the brain in our thoughts, emotions, and behaviors, you will start connecting the dots and you will be better equipped to rewire and reinvent how your brain is working, which subsequently will make you able to define what retirement will look like for you and just you without the pollution from cultural norms or others people's opinions.

LEARNING FROM GUILT, SHAME, AND REGRET

The key question is, how can we access the past that keeps us stuck? Let's explore further how to bring awareness to these areas so we can actually do something about it. We'll explore three types of consequences from past traumas or painful experiences that are frequently encountered, and what to do about them to start healing and move forward.

The first one is guilt. Guilt is a feeling of responsibility or remorse for some offense, wrong, etc., whether real or imagined. Do you feel guilty about something you did or didn't do? Maybe you go through the memories of that event over and over, thinking of what you would have done differently... Guilt may be guiding you as to what you did wrong... I will ask you to think about something you did wrong. Now, I want you to think of other similar situations. Did you react differently? For example, when I was in medical school I got behind in a project because I wanted to spend more time with my friends. I failed that project, and I felt guilt. Ever since that one event I became very mindful of my due dates and developed a higher sense of responsibility. When we sit with our experiences and

our feelings and thoughts, and we actually discover
that we have changed by not repeating what made us
feel guilty initially, we change and heal. This shapes
your person and character.

Here is another example: if you cut off someone in
traffic and they had to stop abruptly, this may have
caused a small accident behind you and you just
kept going... maybe every time you are in traffic you
remember this episode and feel guilty. Recreating
this for healing would look like: being mindful of
other cars while driving and always giving the right
of way to other cars, and being patient in traffic. In
this way, you are healing yourself through changed
behavior. The best apology is to change behavior. So,
guilt can be not that bad. If you feel guilty because
you forgot an appointment, you can apologize and
next time you will be more conscientious of leaving
home earlier.

The second common consequence of trauma is
shame. Shame is an awful feeling, it is unpleasant
and is typically associated with a negative evaluation
of ourselves that makes us hide and feel worthless.
Shame thrives in the darkness, in the secretiveness

of our souls. It makes us not want to speak with others because we are afraid of being judged. It is particularly dangerous because it makes us believe we are "bad" (in contrast to guilt which says "I have done something bad"). It can be the internal motor that is making you want to isolate and spend less time with friends and or family. Perhaps you feel shame because you are not having a good time during your retirement as everyone else was expecting you to do.

The only way to cure shame is to bring it to the light. We cannot permanently prevent shame from affecting us, because shame is natural and comes with being human and how we relate to others. But sharing it with someone in your life who is non-judgmental can help you release the shame that is eating at you at the moment; it can change everything. Maybe we have heard for years messages such as "the cross is carried inside." We collectively believe that vulnerability is a weakness. So, a good place to start working on this is sharing with close friends or family members. Now, you can definitely work on this as you continue to go through the book.

Although shame and guilt may seem similar, they are actually not. The difference is better explained by someone who has dedicated herself to research on shame and vulnerability—Brené Brown, who said during a TED talk:

> Shame is a focus on self, guilt is a focus on behavior. Shame is, 'I am bad.' Guilt is, 'I did something bad.' How many of you, if you did something that was hurtful to me, would be willing to say, 'I'm sorry. I made a mistake'? How many of you would be willing to say that? Guilt: I'm sorry. I made a mistake. Shame: I'm sorry. I am a mistake.

Shame is highly, highly correlated with addiction, depression, violence, aggression, bullying, suicide, and eating disorders. Here's what we need to know even more: Guilt is inversely correlated with those things. The ability to hold something we've done, or failed to do, up against who we want to be is incredibly adaptive. What this means is that when we can learn and improve from our mistakes, we become more adapted to healthy life habits. It's uncomfortable, but it's adaptive. Brené Brown also suggests that guilt has been linked to being prosocial, meaning it is linked to empathy and understanding other perspectives and has relationship-enhancing effects.

And while this has implications for how you will alter the course of your retirement, it is very important to be aware of whom we are surrounding ourselves with. Are you around people who are naturally less shame-prone and more guilt-prone, or the opposite? Who we are will also have effects on how you will live the next years of your life.

The third and last consequence is regret. Regret is when you wish you had done things differently in your past. Often times when thinking about the past we consider all the things we did wrong. I want to challenge you to go a step further in your journaling. For everything you did wrong, add to it what you learned from it. As I said before, the past serves us in two ways: to remember good memories, and to learn from it! The importance of writing is that you are healing as you write.

We all regret things, so a better question to ask is, what advice would you give to your younger self?

Before you continue reading please write down your answers.

Why should we ask this question? Because that advice you are giving to your younger self probably consists of the things you regret not doing or things you stopped doing because of the business of life. That way you are tapping into your inner voice. Now, I want you to change from what advice you would give to your younger self to, "I wish I had..." So, if your advice to your younger self was "go and travel," you then can change it to "I wish I had traveled." Right next to this, write down the reasons why you were not able to do it then. I bet a lot of those barriers are gone now. This is a good way to start paving your new path towards an exciting retirement.

As we return to the topic of your past traumas, I want to conclude with an analogy. If you ever try to save a new file in your computer with the same name as an old file, you will be warned that if you continue you will erase the old one. The new file will replace the old one, and the past file will be erased from the memory. Think of your brain as a human computer and your memories as the files. To overwrite an old file, you have to replace it with a new one. That is what we are doing when we work on our traumas through self-reflection and journaling. If your memory is a mistake, and you rewrite that mistake (either real mistakes or things you perceived as mistakes) as a lesson, that memory becomes a lesson. So right now, you are overwriting past mistakes and rewriting them as lessons. You are editing the same memory that feels like a mistake and editing it into a lesson. This is the process of healing your past. Even if you feel you haven't learned anything from past mistakes, you can do it now. Think about it, then use this analogy and reframe it as a lesson.

Learn Thy Brain

Did I already say that I am totally fascinated by the brain? Even in the scientific and medical field, the brain remains an enigmatic organ. However, with the advances made in the past century, we are getting to know it better. One thing we know today is that the brain has the potential to rewire itself even late in life because of the phenomenon of neuroplasticity. The human brain weighs only three pounds and pretty much controls everything in your body. Without a brain, you cannot move, you cannot breathe. Without a brain you would not be able to have thoughts. So, I am going to spend this section telling you how the brain works and allows us to grow or may keep us stuck.

I will be doing this by discussing two main circuits. The reticular activation system and the limbic system.

THE RETICULAR ACTIVATING SYSTEM (RAS)

The reticular activating system is a bundle of neurons found in your brain and is about the size of your little finger. It acts as a filter and decides which information is important, and which isn't, thus conserving a lot of energy. Some people think that the key to success lies in the reticular activating system. In short, utilizing its full potential can mean the difference between living the life you want and being stuck in a terrible routine, in this case, a terrible retirement. It helps to think of the reticular activating system (RAS) as a filter to what you notice in the world—it's a gatekeeper that lets information get into your conscious mind to pay attention to. Its job is to sort through the massive amounts of information delivered to you by your sensory organs (vision, smell, taste, touch, hearing). Basically, the RAS lets in the information that you are already focused on. When you learn a new word, you keep hearing it everywhere. When you buy a new car, you start seeing it everywhere. This is probably the most common one. This is due to the fact that when you first encountered these things, they left an impression, so now the RAS keeps alerting your brain every time you notice them.

If you believe that you are old and therefore can no longer learn to play a given sport, every time something happens that seems to confirm this belief, the belief becomes stronger. For example, you wake up early in the morning and you trip on the carpet. Immediately this confirms your belief that you are old, clumsy, and slow to react—reasons why you could never learn a new sport. But how many of us—including athletes—have tripped over something throughout our lives? It has nothing to do with age or being retired. Instead, it is your mind making a connection and believing in it. This is just an example.

Can you think of a negative belief you may have about your current situation? Can you write down things that seem to confirm this belief? Just do that, and reflect on it.

The RAS is constantly looking for proof to support your beliefs. If you master controlling the RAS, you may be able to have extreme focus or power to use your mental energy however you want. Essentially, you would be able to choose the "flow" of your energy, just by changing your "focus."

The RAS also controls how you perceive yourself (self-image) and quality of life.

So, if you believe that you are no longer an important member of your family, every time they say or do something that confirms this belief, you will continue to isolate and reinforce this belief. This happens because the RAS works on finding evidence to support the beliefs you hold in your brain, as I have described above. For example, you have a friend always saying "I will get depressed when I retire" because they are focused on that thought. What if you can take that same thought process but change your mindset, your focus, and your belief—instead of thinking you will get depressed, start thinking that you will find joy. Once you do that, you are able to focus on what you want to get which is eventually living a life of abundance. This might sound very simplistic to you, but the neuroscience confirms this system.

The RAS works on what you focus on. Constantly remind yourself about what you can do and what you are able to achieve.

SELF-LIMITING BELIEFS

We started exploring what beliefs are earlier when we discussed mindset. Now I will expand on the notion of *self-limiting* beliefs. Do you have self-limiting beliefs?

Self-limiting beliefs are a collection of opinions of ourselves and others that constrain us in some way. They keep you from seeing the different opportunities presented to you each day and prevent you from seeing your own gifts or accepting the gifts offered to you. The stronger the belief, the more evidence we seem to find to support it, despite the fact that the vast majority of limiting beliefs are simply untrue. Such beliefs are formed unconsciously based on our life experiences and are most often misinterpretations of past events. We cement these beliefs in our minds through repeated thoughts once we have decided that the opinions must be true. The challenge is that holding onto self-limiting beliefs prevents us from taking action. Working through your self-limiting beliefs can have a profoundly positive impact on your self-worth, confidence, and personal empowerment.

You are right now at a crossroads with all the opportunities to rewire your brain. Do you see the relation of the RAS and self-limiting beliefs? If you start changing these beliefs, you will succeed and achieve what you always wanted. Your new mind will start to feel proud and is going to filter the world in a different way because you are training it that way. So basically, this is the scientific explanation as to how the function of the brain makes our mindset and how we can alter that by learning and—mainly—putting in the effort.

For example, I had always wanted to run a half marathon! But I always thought that was absolutely impossible, because I had always been a couch potato and the fact of even doing a 5K was just not possible. So, I started changing my thoughts. And I started setting short-term goals instead of worrying and thinking about all the reasons why I would never be able to do a half marathon. Can you apply this analogy to your current situation? Since you retired, maybe you have been paralyzed by worrying and thinking of the many reasons why this is not working for you. But if it was possible for me, it's possible for you. In a year and a half, I ran four half marathons!!!

It seemed unbelievable, but I did it just by training myself to have new self-beliefs. It was not easy though.

As mentioned before, negative self-beliefs came about because someone in the past either trained you to think this way or because so many bad things happened to you that you trained yourself to believe that bad things will always happen to you or the future is gloomy. So, that became your default mode... (And because we have such a big issue with age discrimination in our society, we tend to think that getting older is equivalent to become frail, unworthy, and not as useful as during our younger years. There are even jobs that would force people to retire only because of their age—and age is only a number. I say all this not to blame anyone but rather to bring it into awareness so we can start implementing change.) "Default mode" is not just a metaphor; in fact, your default mode network is a series of neurons in your brain that is needed because it does not require a lot of thinking. Default mode network refers to the neuronal pathways in charge of executing automatic behaviors. The brain tries to maximize its energy, and by automating behaviors it decreases the need for thinking behaviors through. Take breathing, for example: all the muscles and movements required for breathing do not take thinking effort; they have been optimized for proper functioning. This morning, I am sure you did not think about which hand you would use to eat your breakfast because it is a default. However, some things don't need to be controlled by the default mode network—for example, your self-limiting beliefs. Thinking patterns like "I am going to get depressed when I retire" or "I will not be able to work anymore" have become your default mode, but this is holding you back from achieving your full potential. You can teach yourself to be left handed (if you are not), and this is the same process to change your self-limiting beliefs. It is a process, not an event—we start using thoughts that are positive, optimistic, and fulfilling, and change will take place. This is the only way you can do it. It will help you to move from default mode to really thinking and being present.

THE LIMBIC SYSTEM AND THE PREFRONTAL CORTEX

The limbic system is a circuit in your brain that has to do with past traumatic experiences, and with your innate reaction to anything that might be threatening. It responds to threats and traumas both small and big—from taking your DMV license exam to being in a car accident.

We often think of the past even when we don't realize we do. You may be triggered to remember it by people you see, the places you visit, a song, or even a smell. So many things can trigger a reaction in you, and that is because we have a part of our brain called the amygdala that is in charge of assigning meaning to everything that happens in our life; by the time we get to adulthood, most everything around us has had some type of meaning in our lives and will trigger memories in our brain.

The amygdala is one of the components of the limbic system, which can also be called our emotional brain; it is that part of the brain that responds to a sensory stimulus like a knee-jerk reaction. The prefrontal cortex is that area of the brain which can be called our rational brain. It is this part of the brain that tells you to stop, not to react, and to think through before you react in a way you might regret. It is the part responsible for higher-level thinking processes, and it gets activated when we need to pay sustained attention to a task.

So, if you question the idea of past experiences influencing your thoughts, your reactions and your behaviors today, this is the system in your brain that makes that happen. It is proven.

When a person has experienced negative situations through their lives, or has been told many times that the world is a dangerous place, that person ends up living with a hyper-stimulated limbic system. And when that happens, that person can live in a state of high anxiety. However, as you have lived a busy life, you may have never had the time to feel and process. And when retirement is here and you have lots of time you never had before, those worrying thoughts start to increase and subsequently the anxiety creeps in and everything starts to look scary. That is one of the factors that makes moving into retirement particularly challenging.

The good news is that there are techniques we can use to calm the limbic system. Mainly these have to do with mindfulness. Mindfulness is the psychological process of bringing one's attention to experiences occurring in the present moment. Too much time planning, problem-solving, daydreaming, or thinking negative or random thoughts can be draining. It can also make you more likely to experience stress, anxiety, and symptoms of depression. Practicing mindfulness exercises can help you direct your attention away from this kind of thinking and engage with the world around you. Practicing mindfulness involves breathing methods, guided imagery, and other practices.

I will be focusing on mindfulness meditation. Meditation is exploring. It's not a fixed destination. Your head doesn't become vacuumed free of thought, utterly undistracted. It's a special place where each and every moment is momentous. If you have thoughts coming in and out, that is perfectly ok. The brain produces thoughts, the lungs oxygenate our body. In this practice, you focus on being intensely aware of what you are sensing and feeling in the moment, and you also suspend judgment and approach your experience with warmth and kindness, to yourself and others. This approach can also help unleash your natural curiosity about the workings of your mind.

Why mindfulness meditation? Because it has so many amazing effects on your brain. It causes growth in the prefrontal cortex, which enhances your ability to focus for sustained periods of time. Meditation also decreases hyperactivity of the amygdala (this is the reason why it decreases anxiety, fear, and stress) and increases the volume of another area of the limbic system called the hippocampus, which governs learning and memory.

One last thing: aging causes the brain to shrink. It is just a fact. It is considered normal to a certain extent. However, neuro-imaging studies looking at the brains of people who are expert at meditation versus those who do not meditate has shown that those who meditate slowed age-related brain shrinking. In more medical terms, meditation has been linked to larger amounts of gray matter in the hippocampus and frontal areas of the brain. You already know that the hippocampus creates new memories and the frontal areas of the brain have to do with attention, focus, and complex decision making. Lastly, more gray matter can lead to more positive emotions. A landmark 2005 study by

Harvard neuroscientist Dr. Sara Lazar and colleagues showed that the brains of meditators had remarkably more "thickness," "folds," and overall "surface area" in their left prefrontal cortexes, which is a location in the brain connected to positive emotions.[5] It turns out that meditation is pretty awesome!

This is as medical or scientific as I am going to get in this book. But I don't want to leave this here before asking you to start a new habit. I'm sure you know that it is to start meditating. If you already meditate, that is great! There are many types of meditation, and there are also many ways you can help yourself start this new practice. One example is smartphone apps. My favorite one is called Headspace, but there are many others out there. You can also check to see if there are places where they do group meditation in your community.

[5] Available at: https://www.ncbi.nlm.nih.gov/pmc/articles/PMC1361002/

HOW TO START A MEDITATION PRACTICE

Sit comfortably, on a cushion with your legs crossed in front of you or on a chair with your feet planted on the floor.

Straighten your upper body without making it stiff. Place your arms parallel to your upper body and rest the palms of your hands on your legs or wherever feels most comfortable to you.

You can close your eyes, or you may choose not to do that. Either way is good.

Start feeling how you are breathing and bring all your attention to this. Notice the air going through your nostrils all the way to the bottom of your lungs. Notice your chest or belly rising and falling. Your mind will wander away from your breath—that is inevitable. And when you notice this, bring your attention gently back to the breathing process.

You may want to close your eyes now. Start noticing the noise around you, how your body feels, your thoughts and feelings. You can stay here as little or as long as you please. Just make sure it is natural and not forced. It can be 3 minutes, or it can be 10 minutes. Then open your eyes.

Grab your journal and write down your experience with this short process. This will be just your beginning into mindfulness meditation.

SMART Goal-setting

Now that we have learned how the brain works, let's dive into some action. We are going to take a ride down a path that will lead us into the development of SMART goals.

It all starts with talking about control. Control is a very important aspect of human optimization to understand, which is really what we want to do while you continue this work on your new life as a retired person. More importantly, knowing what is 100-percent under your control and, conversely, what is not 100-percent under your control is what matters. Let's explore first what is not under your control.

Make a list of all the things that come to your mind that aren't fully under your control.

The list can go on, I bet. Some things that are included in this category will include the weather, and associated contingencies; illness; opportunities. And a big one for most people: other people's opinions of you. The fear of what others think of you is so common and pervasive, to the point that I would say it paralyzes many people. But let's face it, what others think of you has nothing to do with who you are (unless you let it define you, and then you can definitely lose control of your own life). What others think of you is merely their own "belief" about you, and we have already defined what beliefs are.

Let us look at what is 100-percent under your control. Can you name a few?

What is under your control falls mainly into two groups: thoughts and actions (or, attitudes and effort). Thoughts and actions make up the essence of you. This is what you need to master. You need to connect to the things that are 100-percent under your control, train them, master them. This will lead to thoughts that will serve you.

CONTROL AND GOALS

Have you thought about why we spend so much time planning for the future? Setting goals? Our frontal lobe is designed to do this. We are drawn to it and enjoy the process. The most important reason why the brain insists on doing this is so that we can take control of our lives, or at least feel a degree of control. We look into the future so that we can take action and make it happen. Every great thing out there was first imagined and visualized before it became great; the Great Wall of China was first planned out, the Mona Lisa first was imagined... Tesla cars, airplanes, iPhones, video games, Disneyland, anything that you can think of was first an idea in someone's head.

> " Imagination is everything. It is the preview of life's coming attractions."
> —Albert Einstein

You are 100-percent, totally and completely in control of your life. You get to choose what you do, what you eat (or don't eat), who you spend time with, if you are disciplined (or not). You choose what you spend time thinking about, what you worry about (or don't worry about). You choose to choose or not to choose, and truth be told, not choosing is also a choice.

You are the architect of your own life, and when you become aware of this, a whole new world of perspectives opens up. This goes back to the growth mindset, when you believe that you have infinite potential and realize that the keys are in your hands, the future suddenly looks much brighter. What is between you and the amazing future you dream of is a set of skills that you can obtain. It may be hard work, but you can own your life, get the skills you need, and learn the things you need to learn.

So many times, I hear people describing all the reasons why they can't. This is "learned helplessness" that ties their hands. "I can't do it because I have no money," "I can't because I am too old for that." The idea that only a few lucky ones were born to succeed is nonsense. Great choices and actions lead to great lives, lousy choices and actions lead to a lousy life. You choose and define your destiny, your future. Your life should reflect your choices.

Let us do an exercise. Write down the top three most important things or people in your life.

Now, think back on your last week's schedule—how much time did you spend on these things or with these people? Is there a gap between what you state is your priority and what you actually practice?

A thriving and successful life depends on hope. Not the type of hope that expects tomorrow will be a better day, but the type of hope that leads to actions. The type of hope that has the expectation that our own efforts can improve our future. "I have a feeling that tomorrow will be better" is different from "I resolve to make tomorrow better." The former is passive, while the latter is active. The hope that successful people have has nothing to do with luck and everything to do with getting up again.

You have to set goals and then turn those goals into actions.

> *A dream written down with a date becomes a goal. A goal broken down into steps becomes a plan. A plan backed by action makes your dreams come true."*
>
> *—Greg Reid*

Bottom line: a goal needs to be followed by a plan of action, otherwise you will just remain stuck in daydreaming. The way you set goals is very important. Goal setting requires focus and consistent action. Goals are part of every aspect of life. No matter where you look, you are setting goals—consciously or unconsciously. It might be a relationship (a goal to get closer, to communicate better, etc.), it might be your health, it might be how you are going to fill up your time or maybe go back to work or volunteer, or perhaps help with grandkids, or even the way you will recover.

Your daily actions, your goals and choices, must be consistent with your values and life philosophy. Let's explore your personal values.

WHAT ARE VALUES? WHY DO THEY MATTER?

Values are part of us. Values determine what is most important for you. They are what you stand for, what you live for. They can represent your uniqueness. They guide your behavior, decisions, and actions. When you know your values, you can live and make decisions according to your values. When we honor our values, we find fulfillment. The problem is that if you don't know what your values are, you may unintentionally violate your values on a daily basis with the decisions you make, and with your behavior. So, what is the problem if this is not intentional? Well, violating your values creates inner tension that leads to varying degrees of feeling uncomfortable in your own skin. This in turn can lead to unhealthy habits or unhealthy ways of coping with the uncomfortable feelings (for example, you may cope with uneasy feelings by drinking or eating, working on a project that is a step to something bigger but not necessarily what you enjoy, etc.).

'Cheshire Cat,' asked Alice. 'Would you tell me please, which way I ought to go from here?'
'That depends a good deal on where you want to go,' said the Cat.

'I don't much care where,' said Alice.
'Then it doesn't matter where you go,' said
the Cat."

—Lewis Carrol

Most of us don't know our core values and instead focus on what society expects of us, or what our neighbors think of us, or what we think we should do or become. It is easy to idealize what values we should pick or stand for. The truth is that knowing what your values are is key to happiness. Joy comes from doing work or activities that are aligned with your core values. When you do activities that are not aligned with your values, you feel uneasy and become discouraged more easily. Today, we will be working on unearthing your values, discovering them...

Before we get to the actual exercise, you will see an extensive list of values. This is to get you thinking about what values are. Probably most of them will sound appealing to you. The goal is not for you to pick one but for you to be familiarized with what we mean when we talk about values. They are there just to prime you into thinking about what is coming next.

VALUES

Accomplishment	Ease
Accuracy	Effortlessness
Acknowledgement	Empowerment
Adventure	Enthusiasm
Authenticity	Environment
Beauty	Excellence
Calm	Focus
Collaboration	Freedom
Community	Friendship
Compassion	Fun
Comradeship	Generosity
Confidence	Gentleness
Connectedness	Growth
Contentment	Happiness
Contribution	Harmony
Cooperation	Health
Courage	Helpfulness
Creativity	Honesty
Curiosity	Humor
Determination	Idealism
Directness	Independence
Discovery	Integrity

Joy
Kindness
Learning
Love
Loyalty
Orderliness
Participation
Partnership
Passion
Patience
Peace
Productivity
Respect
Romance
Self-Esteem
Service
Simplicity
Spirituality
Spontaneity
Strength
Tact
Thankfulness
Tolerance
Tradition

Trust
Understanding
Unity
Vitality

So, let's do an exercise. First, I will ask you to clear your mind, take a deep breath, and have an open mind. The answers will not come from your conscious mind; the answers do not need to be reasoned. Go with what comes first. Writing it down on paper is very helpful to let the thoughts flow.

The first thing you will do is write a list of 20–30 values/words that best describe you. Again, pick words that fit you, and not what others would expect of you, or how you would like to be perceived. You can use the list that was provided, or search on the internet for a similar list.

The following prompts will help guide you towards the right ones:

- *Think of a time when you felt at your best (personally, professionally, etc.)—a meaningful experience. Now, take time to answer the following questions: What were you doing at this time? What was happening to you? What values were you honoring?*
- *Think of a time when you got very angry or upset, and take time to answer the following*

questions: What was going on? What were your feelings? What value is being suppressed?
· *Think of what is most important to you; what brings fulfillment to your life today?*

You can do these exercises with different experiences. Now, combine all the words/values that came up after doing the prior exercises and build a list. Maybe the list will have about 20–40 values. The next step will be to group them together in clumps of related values. For example, the following values are related to each other: Achievement — Accomplishment — Greatness — Professionalism — Success.

Once you have separated the words into groups of related values, you will select the word that best represents that group and highlight it. You may still have a large number of values on the list. As you are consolidating the list, it may get harder and harder to identify what best defines you. These questions may help with narrowing it down even more:

· *What values are essential to your life?*
· *What values are a good representation of your way of being?*

· *What values best support your inner self?*

These questions can help you identify what really goes on your list. There is no magic number of values you should be left with. If there are too few, you may be missing key values that are core to your essence. If there are too many, it will be hard to get the most out of them for our purpose. We will work with the goal of having between four and eight.

Once you are down to four to eight words that best describe the values you hold dear to your heart, the next step will be to put them in ranking order of importance. Let this sink in for a day or two, and you may consider revisiting the ranking order to see how you feel about it and if the order of importance needs rearranging.

Once you have reviewed the list, creativity can be helpful to make them even more meaningful to you. After each value, write down a sentence describing what that value means for you. For example, I will share with you some of my values and how I define them:

- *Authenticity: knowing that we are true to ourselves without masks or pretending to be someone else*
- *Adventure: to have fun and to explore*
- *Spirituality: to have meaning in life that comes from serving a higher power*

SETTING GOALS BASED ON YOUR VALUES

The final step will be to create some goals for your retirement. I have been sharing with you the importance of values and a personal philosophy because this goes hand in hand with your goals. But there is a difference between values and goals:

- Goals have a desired result, usually in the future—things we want to achieve or do.
- Values are principles or standards of behavior, a guide to life. Values live in the present moment and can provide a deep sense of direction for life when thoughts and actions are aligned with them.

Let's explore SMART goals. SMART goals are a structured way of setting goals that align with your core values, that will help you get a step closer to your life vision.

It helps to create a verifiable trajectory towards a certain objective rather than toward vague resolutions.

Even though this is not the definition of SMART, when I see this acronym, what comes to my mind is Simple,

Meaningful ART. Because even though this looks pretty simple, it takes art to make these types of goals real and at the end of the day will help you give meaning to your life.

SMART stands for:

- **Specific:** What exactly do you want to achieve? The more specific you get, the better. This step helps clarify a vague goal such as "I want to enjoy my retirement" into something more specific like: "I want to go on a camping trip this summer with my family so I can enjoy the next month." Questions that might help include: What do I want? Where? How? When? With whom? Any limitations? Why? Alternatives?

- **Measurable:** What are you going to use to determine if you meet the goal? It provides a way to measure progress. So, for the case above, you may want to set weekly goals until the trip happens.

- **Achievable:** Is it attainable? In this step, you measure time, effort, and costs your goal will take against the profits and other obligations and priorities you have currently. Aiming big is good—you should "shoot for the stars, and you might land in the moon"—but also consider that if you actually are shooting for the moon, your goal might not actualize. So, if you are not going to have time to prepare for your camping trip, you'll certainly fail, and all your negative self-beliefs will focus on all the ways retirement is bad.

· **Relevant:** The main question here is why. Why do you want to achieve this goal? If the answer aligns with your values, you are on the right track.

· **Timely:** This is where you set a timeline. Set small steps towards your goal, steps that are realistic.

SMART is an effective tool to provide clarity, focus, and motivation to help you achieve your goals as you transition and overall as you continue your journey as a retiree. I encourage you to go online and search for a SMART worksheet, or create one of your own.

PILLAR 3:
Social

Friends

Are you feeling lonely? Has it been more difficult for you to find ways to build networks or maintain in a healthy state those that you already have? What you are going to learn in this chapter is crucial for a successful retirement. But I do not want you to start thinking that now you will have to go out there and meet all these people when you have never been like that. No, that is not the case. Remember that whatever you take from this book on how to shift your retirement experience to one of freedom and joy, must be 100-percent aligned with your values, with who you are. There are people that by nature are totally extroverted, and then we have those on the other side of the spectrum who are totally introverted.

Let's explore this spectrum of personality traits. Yes, it is a spectrum and you can be either on one end or somewhere in between. On the surface, introverts are quiet and private, and extroverts are talkative and outgoing. But many introverts can be outgoing and talkative. I am one of those. And the opposite is true for extroverts. This is how you can find out where you fit better. Introverts recharge by spending time alone. Yes! There is no problem with being alone if you enjoy that and if it makes you recharge your energy. Introverts also enjoy small conversations, they have closer relationships and just a few friends. Introverts have a tendency to listen more. They are private and will open up only to very close people. Now, extroverts recharge by being social, they enjoy large group conversations and have more friends but the relationships are sometimes less strong. They speak more, are more open, and love getting attention. So, where do you fit?

Feeling lonely at this stage is more common than you may think. And despite this, no one wants to admit to being lonely. Most likely you have not spoken about this. A recent survey by Granset, the over-50s social networking site, found that almost three-quarters of older people in the UK are lonely and most have never spoken to someone about how they feel. It also discovered that about 70 percent said their close friends and family would be surprised if they said they were lonely.[6] The change from interacting with people

[6] Available at: https://nypost.com/2017/08/07/loneliness-is-a-greater-health-risk-than-obesity-study-says/

at work constantly, or from all the interactions you had raising kids, is now suddenly gone and that can make you feel isolated. Retirement comes as a big shock to who you are.

There are many reasons to feel lonely in retirement. Getting sick—this can make it more difficult to leave the house. Relocation—either you move, or all your friends are moving away. Or maybe your family is far away. Maybe you are already living a long distance from those who used to be your social support.

Research shows that maintaining social connections is a critical part of healthy aging. In fact, maintaining friendships and family ties may help to reduce the risk of dementia and other age-related illnesses. We are going to learn how to embrace the freedom that retiring gives you as much as you can and consequently will learn the importance of taking the time to discover and experience the things you actually like to do and never had the time to. Go out there and find out what others are doing and join them.

All the time that you have now can make your negative thoughts pop out constantly. Things like "I do not want to be a burden to my family or friends"—which will reinforce this belief that you can be a burden. So, we are going to address this, because we are social beings. This has a lot to do with what you read earlier about meaning and purpose. So, why purpose? What is purpose? It is the intention to contribute to the well-being of others. This is one source of passion and a key component of grit. Grit by definition is passion and perseverance for a long-term and meaningful goal. For most people, purpose is a tremendously powerful source of motivation. Grittier people are dramatically more motivated than others to seek a meaningful, other-centered life.

It is never too late to cultivate a sense of purpose. We will explore exercises that can help you do this.

In your journal answer the following questions:

- *Reflect on how you could contribute to society or your community. How could the world be a better place?*
- *Can you find the connections to anything you might want to do right now?*
- *How can you change your current situation to enhance its connection to your core values?*

Write down even small (but meaningful) ways, which goes toward making a personalized map for what would constitute more meaningful and enjoyable activities. And there are many options for this: reconnecting with friends, making time to meet with them, going for coffee, joining a group for exercise. I once worked with a person who, through his work with me, decided to start joining a group of people that went for walks on Sundays. He was not sure that was what he was going to enjoy but had the interest enough to start doing it. He is now enjoying it and has developed new friends which consequently have given him a purpose. So, take classes, volunteer. This is a great way to find a sense of purpose and happiness because you will be helping those who are less fortunate. There are so many resources for volunteering nowadays. You can also go back to work! There are also options for this. It can be a part time job. Once, I took my car for service and the place had a free van to take clients back home. I was lucky to have a driver that was very talkative. Anyway, he shared with me that he had been recently retired and now has this part-time job. He chose this one in particular because he enjoys talking to people and getting to know them as well as driving.

Find inspiration in a purposeful role model. Imagine yourself 15 years from now: What do you think will be most important to you then? Can you think of someone whose life inspires you to be a better person? Who and why?

But another very important aspect of socialization is with whom we socialize. More important than how much we socialize is the quality of these relations. Motivational speaker Jim Rohn has been attributed a famous quote you may have heard: "You are the average of the five people you spend the most time with."

Research in fact shows that we are more affected by our environment than we think we are. People around us will influence the way we think, the way we make choices, etc.

Nicholas Christakis and James Fowler conducted one of the first major studies on social influence. They were analyzing data from the Framingham Heart Study (one of the largest and longest running health studies ever) when they came across some very interesting information. They were analyzing the effect of family members and friends on something fairly objective:

obesity. What they found is that if you have a friend that becomes obese, you are 45 percent more likely than chance to gain weight over the next two to four years. But that's not all—the interesting part is that if you have a friend of a friend who is obese, you still have a higher chance of gaining weight, now about 20 percent more likely than chance to gain weight. But it does not stop there, if you have a friend of a friend of a friend who develops obesity, you are still 10 percent more likely than random chance to gain weight as well. Through this data they show the impact of relationships in your own life. But it is not only around obesity; this was also the case with smoking. Let's say your friend smokes; this study showed that you are 61 percent more likely to be a smoker yourself. If a friend of your friend smokes you are 29 percent more likely to smoke. And if a friend of a friend of your friend smokes you are still 11 percent more likely to be a smoker.

But you may think, "That is all health related, I'm not sure if that applies." Well, the most telling part was the study on happiness.[7] Research shows that a happy friend will make you happier, and that is no surprise. But if the friend of a friend of your friend is happy with

[7] Available at: https://www.bmj.com/content/337/bmj.a2338

their life, you are 6 percent more likely to be happy yourself. Six percent may not seem like much, but let's put it in contrast with another study that suggests that if I gave you a $10,000 raise, that would only trigger a 2 percent increase in happiness.

So, research definitely supports how those around you can influence you. Why does it matter? Being very intentional about your friends and those around you can have a great impact in your life. You need to know where you sit in the larger context of your social network. You are not just the average of the five people that surround you most of the time, you are an average of a much wider social network.

What about the quality of your friendships? Is it better to have fewer high-quality friends? Or less quality but more quantity?

Vanessa Van Edwards talks about social media friendships (but it does apply to all your friendships).[8] She describes some friends that are "cotton candy friendships," people that are fun to hang with, not so much substance or nutrition there. These are friends

[8] See her website at: https://www.scienceofpeople.com/

you wouldn't call when you need something, they are fun to hang out with from time to time, as cotton candy is good to have from time to time, but if you have too much of it, your teeth began to rot, you get a sugar rush. Eventually you need a meal, more content, more nutrition. The question is, who are the friends that bring nutrition to your life? And who are the friends that are cotton candy? She also talks about the concept of ambivalent friendships. This are people about whom you are not sure—if you like them, if they like you, if you will have fun, etc.... and these are the ones that take the most effort. If there is someone you don't like and they ask you to go to lunch, the answer is easy: "No thanks." But saying no to an ambivalent person is much more difficult. You may or may not like them, or they may or may not like you, so you are much more likely to say yes and take the chance. The problem is that we all like to be liked, and this type of relationship takes much more effort as we want to be liked by them. You have limited mental energy in your day, and if you are spending it in figuring out if someone likes you, that is a waste of time.

The problem becomes how to find out if someone is not a really good friend? Van Edwards proposes one simple question, and although it is simple, it may not necessarily be easy. This is the question: Are you ever doubting that they are really happy for you? (Maybe they often pose passive aggressive comments, or those jokes that really hurt "but they are just jokes," etc.) The truth may hurt, but if you really want to refine the quality of your friendships, you may want to take time to dig deep and answer this question.

Time to do a self-assessment.

List the three people you spend the most time with. For each one of these people, answer the following questions:

- *Write down three to five words that best describe this person.*
- *Think of how they interact and affect you. How do you feel when you are with them, and immediately after?*
- *Do you feel happy and energized after spending time with them? Or do you feel depleted and tired?*
- *How do they support you? In which ways?*

Gratitude

The second aspect of the Social pillar is the attitude of gratitude. Having a constant attitude to be grateful will start making your transition even more blissful. We will take some time to explore why this is so important, and what the neuroscience behind it is.

Gratitude is an amazing, free, and available tool that requires minimal (or no) training or knowledge... and yet despite this, it tends to be frequently overlooked. Sometimes it seems that if it does not cost a lot of effort or money, it is not worth it. Well, we will explore how this is not at all true when it comes to gratitude. Let's explore some of the benefits of gratitude.

It is good for your brain: A National Institutes of Health (NIH) study from 2009 showed that our hypothalamus (the part of the brain that regulates a number of bodily functions such as appetite, sleep, metabolism, growth, etc.) gets activated when we feel gratitude or endorse kindness.[9] Could volunteering give you

---

[9] Available at: https://www.ncbi.nlm.nih.gov/pmc/articles/PMC2733324/pdf/bhn080.pdf

a reward and a higher ability to practice gratitude? I think so!

When experiencing gratitude, the brain releases dopamine. Dopamine is a chemical in your brain that is associated with rewards, and when increased in this way (or by other pleasurable activities such as sex, eating, etc.), it gives us a natural high, a feeling of good experience. A 2005 study demonstrated that keeping a gratitude journal decreased depression by 30 percent while people were involved in the study.[10]

Gratitude improves sleep! As mentioned above, sleep is controlled by the hypothalamus, and since gratitude activates it, it helps make it easier to fall asleep and get better sleep. Because sleep is a basic human need that is connected to many other effects, an improvement in sleep can lead to improvement in depression, pain, stress, anxiety, and it can boost the immune system, as well. Isn't this pretty amazing?

[10] Seligman, M. E. P., Steen, T. A., Park, N., & Peterson, C. (2005). Positive psychology progress: Empirical validation of interventions. American Psychologist, 60, 410–421.

It is good for your body: A study done in 2003 looked at the link between gratitude and pain.[11] People were asked to keep a gratitude journal, and this led to 16 percent experiencing reduced symptoms and 10 percent having a decrease in pain levels.

A study on gratitude showed that people writing in a gratitude journal can (often) reduce blood pressure by 10 percent.[12]

In 1998, there was a research study where subjects were made to cultivate appreciation, and 23 percent showed decreases in cortisol—the most prominent stress hormone—and 80 percent had changes in heart rate variability from reduced stress levels.[13]

[11] J Pers Soc Psychol. 2003 Feb;84(2):377-89. Counting blessings versus burdens: an experimental investigation of gratitude and subjective well-being in daily life. Emmons RA1, McCullough ME.

[12] Available at: https://www.today.com/health/be-thankful-science-says-gratitude-good-your-health-t58256

[13] Integr Physiol Behav Sci. 1998 Apr-Jun;33(2):151-70. The impact of a new emotional self-management program on stress, emotions, heart rate variability, DHEA and cortisol. McCraty R1, Barrios-Choplin B, Rozman D, Atkinson M, Watkins AD.

Being thankful can improve your relationships. A study from 2014 showed that appreciating can help you win new friends, and that thanking a new acquaintance makes them more likely to want an ongoing relationship.[14] Grateful people are more likely to behave in a pro-social manner, enhancing empathy and reducing aggression. A study from the University of Kentucky showed that people who ranked higher in gratitude were less likely to retaliate and were more sensitive and empathetic towards others.[15]

It improves the relationship to yourself—super important! A 2014 study showed that gratitude increased athletes' self-esteem, which is an essential component for optimal performance.[16] Gratitude can help foster resilience and help overcome trauma. This was shown in a study published in 2003 where gratitude was

[14] Available at: https://www.sciencedaily.com/releases/2014/08/140828110810.htm

[15] Available at: https://pdfs.semanticscholar.org/dbe0/35a2eba8aad922f8843ea02a5f5731a6711e.pdf

[16] Chen, Lung & Wu, Chiahuei. (2014). Gratitude Enhances Change in Athletes' Self-Esteem: The Moderating Role of Trust in Coach. Journal of Applied Sport Psychology. 26. 349-362. 10.1080/10413200.2014.889255.

a major contributor to resilience following the 9/11 terrorist attacks.[17]

Many studies have shown that people who consciously count their blessings tend to be happier and less depressed. The findings are amazing: Gratitude can have mental health benefits. The group writing gratitude letters were noted to have a higher percentage of positive emotions and lower rates of negative emotion words than those in the other writing group. What was interesting is that the fewer negative emotion words were associated significantly more with better mental health in individual reports. Perhaps writing grateful thoughts makes it harder to ruminate on negative experiences. It may not necessarily be a fast response, but it definitely is a lasting one. The research also showed that the effects of gratitude where not noticeable within the first week, but were noticeable 4 weeks after, and had lasting effects even 12 weeks after. Another study using fMRI showed that people participating in gratefulness showed greater

[17] Fredrickson, B. L., Tugade, M. M., Waugh, C. E., & Larkin, G. R. (2003). What good are positive emotions in crises? A prospective study of resilience and emotions following the terrorist attacks on the United States on September 11th, 2001. Journal of personality and social psychology, 84(2), 365–376.

neural sensitivity in the medial prefrontal cortex, the area implicated with decision making and complex cognitive behavior, among other functions. And this greater activation in the medial prefrontal cortex was shown to be present three months later as well, indicating lasting effects that a gratitude journal practice can have.

Much of our time is spent pursuing things that we currently don't have, worrying about the future. Gratitude reverses this process to help us focus on the present, to help us appreciate the people and things we do have right now.

Now, I urge you to begin a gratitude journaling practice.

The next time you wake up in the morning, write in your journal two things you are grateful for. That way you will start setting the tone for the day. And then, right before bed, grab your journal and write one thing you are grateful for from the day that just passed. In 30 days, review your journal and you will see all of those amazing things you experienced in the past 30 days.

PILLAR 4:
Spiritual

As humans, we have an innate desire or drive to worship (connect to something higher than ourselves). It can be God, but it also can be money, power, a famous person, or oneself. But everyone worships something. Some might call this a drive for meaning or purpose—a looking outside of oneself for a frame of orientation, for something that gives focus, meaning, purpose, and understanding to life. The question is not, do we worship? But rather, what are we worshiping? We adapt ourselves to the things we admire and devote ourselves to the things we idealize. In psychiatry this is called modeling.

Man Searching for Meaning

> " What matters, therefore, is not the meaning of life in general but rather the specific meaning of a person's life at a given moment..."
>
> —Viktor Frankl

Meaning, what is the meaning of life, at this stage what is the meaning of your life? Let me introduce you to a man who lived a life of meaning. A person who was so devoted to this thing called life. At this stage of your life, you have been exposed to adversity. We only need to be alive to face problems, challenges, and difficulties. Some people have it better than others, but we also share bad outcomes. The reality is that adversity mostly is out of our control. But there is something else that will always be under our control regardless of what is going on in our lives. We will come back to this.

The man I am referring to is Viktor Frankl. Frankl earned a medical degree from the University of Vienna Medical School in 1930. In 1942, Frankl was deported to a Nazi concentration camp along with his wife, parents, and other family members. He was the only member of his family to survive. In 1945, he returned to Vienna and published a book on his theories, based on his records of observations during his time in the camps, called *Man's Search for Meaning*. You may or may not be familiar with his work. This book has been quoted by multiple highly successful individuals as one of the books that impacted their growth.

Dr. Frankl developed a therapy known as logotherapy, which in essence states that the pursuit of meaning or the will to meaning is the primary motivator in humans, not the pursuit of pleasure or the pursuit of power or even the pursuit of happiness. When someone fails to find meaning in life, they turn to find pleasure or power—in order to fill the void that the absence of meaning has left in them. Now, I want to be clear on this, by sharing these principles I am not intending to do any type of therapy, I just want you to be informed and knowledgeable in a way of seeing and feeling the world and life that brings change and growth. Individuals did not create the meaning; rather, meaning is discovered through every living moment and a change of attitude is required in order to discover it. Meaning presents in different ways to each individual. We all face different situations in our lives. No matter what fate brought, if one took appropriate action and adopted the right attitude to the situation, a meaningful life could be realized. And this, my readers, is that one thing that we can always control—our attitude. Dr. Frankl has many powerful quotes; one of them is, "Everything can be taken from a man but one thing: the last of the human freedoms—to choose one's attitude in any given set of circumstances, to choose one's own way."

One should not search for an abstract meaning of life. Everyone has their own specific vocation or mission in life to carry out a concrete assignment which will align with one's values and purpose. One way to do this is to find your own vocation. As quoted by Dr. Frankl from Friedrich Nietzsche: "He who has a why to live for can bear almost any how."

Isn't this a major barrier for freedom during retirement? Perhaps you are feeling that now that you are not doing what you did for decades then life has no purpose to you, and the meaning has been lost. Perhaps you feel that your children are all adults and with busy lives, so you are no longer important to them. Where is your identity now? Who are you? There are so many amazing ways to create a new meaning or maybe just tweak your own definition of what is meaningful to you. According to Dr. Frankl, we can discover this meaning in life in three different ways:

- By creating a work or doing a deed. What comes to mind for you?
- By experiencing something or encountering someone. Perhaps there is something you never had the chance to experience in the first decades of your life. I can think of a couple of them, but it really has to come from within you. I worked with a person who, long ago, started writing children's books but never had time to finish or publish them. After we worked together, she brought them back to life and started looking for publishing companies. She saw the light within this transition in her life.
- By the attitude we take toward unavoidable suffering. You choose the attitude you take toward the sudden death of a loved one, having a severe debilitating illness, losing most of your

retirement money over medical treatment, and so on. The list can go on and on.

His theory is based on a set of assumptions. One of them is that we are free to activate our will to find meaning and this can be done under any circumstances. This deals with the change of attitudes. Another assumption is the meaning of the moment, which is more practical in daily living than an ultimate meaning and is something that is in constant flow rather than set in stone. Unlike ultimate meaning, this meaning-in-the-moment can be found and fulfilled. This can be done by following the values of society or by following the voice of our conscience.

Since meaning is so personal and it should be different for each of you, let's put this concept into practice. How might you apply the principles of Dr. Frankl's work to improve your everyday life and be more fulfilled starting now?

· *Create something. Write down something you once created and write next to it the emotions(s) you experienced. Write down something you had wanted to create but have*

*not and set a goal for that. What is keeping
you from doing it? Knowing what you know
now, how are you going to make it happen?*
· *Develop relationships. Volunteer. I worked
with someone who decided one day she was
going to volunteer with a non-profit providing
breakfast on the weekends to the homeless
in her area. Never did she imagine that
this one experience was going to bring so
much meaning and purpose. She just did it
because someone had challenged her. Have
you volunteered? Have you randomly made
an act of kindness? If yes, write down the
experience, the emotions attached, and what
was meaningful about it to you. Spending time
with others will help you to develop a sense of
meaning in your life.*
· *Find purpose in pain. If you are going through
something bad, try to find a purpose in it.
Even if this is a bit of mental trickery, it will
help to see you through. Or write down a
moment in your past where you experienced
adversity. Today, try to look back to find the
meaning in that pain and write it down.*
· *Focus on others. Try to focus outside of*

yourself to get through feeling stuck about a situation. Travel, experience other cultures, and get to know people from different walks of life. Connect through stories. Accept the worst. When you go out seeking the worst, it reduces the power that it has over you. Prepare for the worst, expecting the best as many have said.

Now remember: Understand that life is not fair. However, life can always have meaning, even in the worst of situations. You might feel that right now in your life things may not be fair for you. While life is not fair, you do have the freedom to find meaning. Remember that you are always free to make meaning out of your life situation. Nobody can take that away from you. This is where your power lies.

Meaning has everything to do with the spiritual life of a person. And we know that spirituality is an absolute part of people's lives.

Don't Stop Me Now

Yes! Don't let your brain stop you now. Those negative thoughts will come out, it is natural to resist change, and this book is all about change. No matter how it feels, just keep doing the work.

Think of how diamonds are formed. They are unique because of the special conditions that create them. They are put under a lot of pressure at very high temperatures. When carbon-bearing ore is exposed to these high temperatures, the carbon is then transformed into a diamond. Exactly like that, our own process of growth and change needs to go through intense work and perseverance. When you start feeling that you want to go back to your old ways, that is when you actually need to keep going on. Schedule some time, think of it as if you are going to meet someone, and that someone is you. You wouldn't not show up for a scheduled meeting, right? Well, this scheduled meeting with yourself is equally if not more important than any other meeting. Practice, because practice leads to mastery.

Think of this book as the foundation for your new home. Your new home now is your retirement. This home had a foundation, but knowing that you will be here for a while, you decided to invest and make it stronger to keep you and your loved ones safe in the comfort of a peaceful mind and to seek shelter during rough weather.

Reading this book and journaling along was all part of the process and of learning. Now you have so much that you are aware of. In order to get unstuck in a state of worries and feelings of sadness or anxiety you have to be willing to put in the work. There are going to be problems; they have always been there. And some of them you are not going to be able to solve and I will not solve them for you, and neither will anyone else. It is all that inner growth that will pay off. Not everyone can do this. As you have felt through these four pillars, it is hard! It is hard to change your mindset. It is hard to start getting attuned to your feelings and sit with them, letting them be. It is natural to experience a lot of internal resistance. Remember when we talked about the brain pathways and how we can change those routes? Well, that takes time. Remember when we discussed about goals, values, and philosophy?

Well, it takes action, perseverance, passion, and—
bottom line—courage. Change is daily, is a state of
constant flow.

And if during this process life challenges you and
something happens, be kind to yourself. Use your skills
from recovery; sleep well—don't sacrifice that. Eat well
and go out in nature; spend some time surrounding
yourself with nature and you will be adding value to
your day. Or if you already have an exercise routine,
go ahead and work out—ride a bike, swim, whatever
it is. It is going to clear your thoughts. Meditate—that
will calm down your thoughts and will change how
your brain is wired. And then go to that meeting you
made with yourself and keep putting in the effort. It
will pay off.

You have tools, you have awareness, you did exercises,
but it is not over. You are going to enter a honeymoon
period with all the work you have put in. But that is
not going to last. Because that is what life is, it flows,
it moves, it does not wait. So, the work must continue
every day of your life. Never cease to grow. As an
extra perk you can now understand the underlying
brain circuits that control our thinking and you have

ways to shift negative thoughts about retirement into positive ones. You are one step SMARTer as you learned to set up smart goals that align with your philosophy and your values.

You can become an ambassador to people like you. You can be creative and find many different ways to do so. You can lead by example, and you can start a domino effect with people who are going through the same transition. Spread the word. Perhaps, you can help people get healthier. It is not a secret that as we get older we can get sicker. But that is not necessarily true. A part of this is also in your hands. Subsequently you have discovered the power of the "pursuit of meaning" the importance to start finding meaning today and that you are not alone. That many people are walking the same walk.

This has made it easier for you to develop habits that will keep you engaged with your friends, family, and community at large, giving you purpose and preventing loneliness. You are not defined by your age. Any age is a good opportunity to start new things. To develop new projects and to build new relations. What a great way to give back to the world! You will be the best at that. You have experienced what it is to be "freaking out" and you have overcome that. That makes you the expert. So, don't stop now. Growth is constant; focus on the process and not on the outcome. Forget about the expectations and live one day at a time.

Remember that great choices and actions lead to great lives. You choose and define your destiny, your future. You already made that choice now keep it up! Your life should reflect your choices. Now you can do the things that are so meaningful to you, those that align to your values, without been impacted by all the negative stuff you heard about retirement. Without worrying about other people's opinions or what their expectations were about you. You can do this by being freeing and true to yourself.

You have a new present, and that is a retirement where freedom is at the core and you are empowered with better tools to overcome difficulties as they arise. And as Dr. Seuss said: "Congratulations! today is your day. You're off to great places, you're off and away! And will you succeed? Yes! you will, indeed!"